THE FURNITURE STYLES

THE
FURNITURE STYLES

BY

HERBERT E. BINSTEAD

EDITOR
" THE FURNITURE RECORD AND THE FURNISHER "

Design may be considered to be of various degrees according to its originality, which is that quality that distinguishes it from the mere repetition of previously arranged forms. . . . Design may be described as the embodiment of thought.—JOHN LEIGHTON.

JM
CLASSIC EDITIONS

This edition digitally re-mastered and
published by JM Classic Editions © 2007
Original text © Herbert E Binstead 1904

ISBN 978-1-905217-30-4

CONTENTS

ILLUSTRATIONS

ILLUSTRATIONS

ILLUSTRATIONS

ILLUSTRATIONS

THE FURNITURE STYLES

CHAPTER I

THE ELIZABETHAN STYLE

To all practical intents and purposes, we may regard what is commonly recognized as the Elizabethan style as the commencement of style in furniture in this country. Although for perhaps half a century before Elizabeth's reign, sideboards and cabinets (and certainly chairs) had reached England from Italy, Germany, and Holland, they can hardly be said to have taken the form of a " style " until the era of " Good Queen Bess," in the second half of the sixteenth century. For a long time England had been " feeling after " something better in the way of decorative furniture. In the reign of Henry VIII that monarch, in an endeavour to make his palaces more magnificent, had brought over from Italy native workmen, and many Dutch craftsmen and artists were also induced to come to this country with the same object. It is to Elizabeth's reign, however, that we must attribute the earliest signs of real development. The Elizabethan period was a time of awakening in many directions, and decorative work moved rapidly upward in sympathy with the other *beaux arts*. Under the ever ready patronage of the Queen, the heavy Gothic designs were promptly superseded. Doubtless there were not wanting in those days objectors to the innovations, and we know that some Elizabethan forms were denounced as " frivolous." Nevertheless the change was a welcome one, and stately solemnity was forced to yield to considerations of utility, if not of actual comfort, and articles were designed with some reference to their usefulness as well as their solidity. The outlines were largely Dutch, but richly ornamented by carving, and the combination makes up the distinctive features of Elizabethan furniture.

At this time smaller rooms appear to have become popular. Sometimes the prevailing big apartments were divided

FIG. 1. ELIZABETHAN SIDEBOARD

by screens, and carving was used in all directions, and was very elaborate. Walls were panelled with carved woodwork, carved picture and mirror frames were freely used, and fluted columns and pilasters were extremely popular. Sometimes the wall decoration would be varied by the carved panelling being shortened to a wainscot, over which tapestry would be hung. At this time rich fabrics were being imported in considerable quantities and provided the furnishers of that

2

day with material for a variety of results. Italy was supplying velvets and damasks, whilst from Holland came tapestries. The time of France was not yet in this particular, and it was not until over half a century later that the great Gobelins' factory was established. It is not surprising that

FIG. 2. ELIZABETHAN CHEST

subsequently an extravagant luxuriousness was developed. In other directions an excess of magnificence prevailed, and some of the furniture of the time reflects the passing mood. If, as is recorded, a suit worn by a nobleman was sometimes equal in value to his whole estate, what wonder that vulgarity of the same nature should influence the manufacture of furniture.

The chairs of this period (apart from upholstered chairs imported from Holland) had carved oak frames and loose cushions for seats. Typical of the style, too, are the massive

3

carved oak bedsteads and chests similarly adorned. The pre-eminent feature of the style is its carving. Taught their art by the Dutch woodcarvers, the English workmen soon eclipsed the foreigner, and we have the result in what may be fairly called an English style, whilst freely admitting the extent of the foreign influence.

The typical features of Elizabethan carving were scroll ornaments of intricate design, armorial bearings, and allegorical figures. Carpets were as yet only available for the rich, and even then were only used to cover tables. In the poorer dwellings the tapestry hangings for the walls gave place to a kind of cheap painted canvas, " decorated " with verses or mottoes. An example of these can be seen in the South Kensington Museum bearing the following verse—

> Read what is written on the painted cloth,
> Do no man wrong, be good unto the poor;
> Beware the mouse, the maggot and the moth,
> And ever have an eye unto the door.

Time changes many things, but twentieth century men will find the injunctions contained in that verse not inappropriate to their own age.

The later Elizabethan style is most ornate, articles being gilded and painted in bright colours, by no means always satisfying to the artistic taste. It is difficult, naturally, to look at these things as the men of the sixteenth century looked at them, but the prices obtained for genuine pieces of this period compare very unfavourably with the prices fetched by choice expressions of the cabinet-maker's art of a couple of centuries later. Even distance fails to lend enchantment to the view in the case of some old furniture. It is not too much to say that a great deal of the furnishing of the time was marked by mere ostentatious display, and often has little merit other than the somewhat questionable one of great costliness. Thus we read of carpets bordered

4

FIG. 3. ELIZABETHAN CABINET

with a trimming largely composed of pearls, and that not an isolated example. In 1574 Queen Elizabeth appears to have found it necessary to protest against the extravagance in this direction, as well as in dress. In a proclamation she

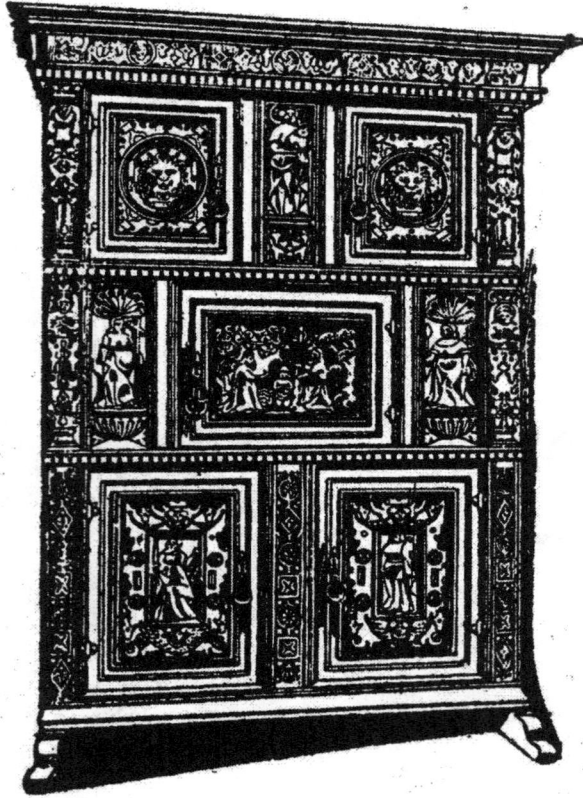

FIG. 4. EARLY ELIZABETHAN BUFFET

speaks of " the superfluitie of unnecessarye foreign wares," which is declared to have " growen by sufferance to such an extremetie, that the manifest decay, not only of a great part of the wealth of the whole realme generally, is like to follow by bringing into the realme such superfluities of silkes, cloths

6

of gold, sylver and other most vaine devices, of so greate coste for the quantitie thereof." Aimed primarily at the importation of foreign goods, because, " as of necessitie the moneyes and treasure of the realme is, and must be, yeerely conveyed out of the same," this proclamation was followed,

FIG. 5. ELIZABETHAN STAIRCASE DECORATIONS

six years later, by a more stringent one still. Such was the extravagant note of the times.

Having said that, it must be admitted that the furniture industry made great advance in this progressive reign. And still more noteworthy is the fact that now for the first time comfortable furniture commences to grace the homes of the people. Not, of course, that any but the fairly well-to-do yet enjoyed much in this direction, but the student of history will note, as Green puts it—

The life of the Middle Ages concentrated itself in the vast castle hall, where the baron looked from his upper dais on the retainers who gathered

7

at his board. . . . The whole feudal economy disappeared when the lord of the household withdrew with his family into his " parlour " or " withdrawing-room " and left the hall to his dependents.

From which beginnings has come the modern British home.

We have already referred to the tendency toward smaller

FIG. 6. ELIZABETHAN STAIRCASE DECORATIONS

rooms, but the term " smaller " is used only in a relative sense as compared with the large halls and apartments of the preceding period. For modern purposes, the style is not very suitable, requiring, as it does, buildings of an extensive character. It was designed for the homes of nobles, not for the common people, and was eminently suited to its purpose.

8

It has been said that the Elizabethan is a midway stage between the " uncomfortable public art of the Gothic and the homelike Georgian. In the Gothic no one had comfort. In the Elizabethan the great built for their own ease, while the common people lived much as before. In the Georgian comfort was found to be a possibility in the homes of the

FIG. 7. ELIZABETHAN CARTOUCHE

middle and lower classes." By free adaptation, however, the style has been made productive of some quite charming schemes of furnishing and decoration, even when applied to houses of small proportions. In Elizabeth's reign, be it noted, the lower middle class were not " consumers " of furniture to any extent, and their dwellings contained only the roughest benches and tables. Still, from this time we may trace a steady " growth downward " in the extension of art and comfort in the homes of the people. The rude farmhouses were superseded by decent buildings of brick

9

and stone, and the furnishing of these dwellings naturally moved in sympathy. At this time the chimney corner was originated, chimneys coming into use during this reign. These, and many other small things, indicate the great movement that had started, and that was to proceed unchecked until the comfortable British home should have become an accomplished fact.

CHAPTER II

THE QUEEN ANNE STYLE

THE style in furniture designated, for the sake of convenience, the Queen Anne, is not, to be accurate, strictly contemporaneous with the reign of the Queen of that name.
It is, of course, always more or less difficult to divide one
period from another closely following or preceding it; and,

FIG. 8. QUEEN ANNE STOOL

speaking generally, the furniture ordinarily described as
Queen Anne may be taken to be that produced during the
last few years of the seventeenth and the first decade of the
eighteenth century. That period, of course, includes the
reign of William and Mary, and it is questionable whether,
indeed, we have not to go still farther back, even into the
time of the unhappy James II, if we would get at the real
beginnings of the peculiar characteristics recognized under
the broad description of Queen Anne.

The exaggeration of Jacobean ornament about the time
of James II prepared the way, in a measure, for a less rococo
style, and many of the Queen Anne pieces indicate, in their

11

almost austere abstention from anything like florid decoration, something akin to a protest against what had gone before. The fact must be admitted, however, that the style we know as Queen Anne did not originate in this country, but was the effect of influence from abroad. William of Orange was Stadtholder of the United Netherlands, and

FIG. 9. QUEEN ANNE CHEST OF DRAWERS

upon his accession a number of skilled Dutch craftsmen found their way to this country, which was not at all surprising. To the work of these men, coupled no doubt with the general desire to escape from the excess of the later Jacobean designs, is due the origin of the Queen Anne style. Thus the Queen Anne style signifies something more than any one idea, and is due to several causes. In it we have, clearly traceable, the old order passing, giving place to the new, and that is why we urge that for a full and complete

12

explanation of the style we must take into our reckoning a period dating from the reign of James II down to at least the year of the death of Anne—1714.

It is not uninteresting to note that though the Queen Anne period is contemporaneous with that of Louis Quatorze

FIG. 10.
QUEEN ANNE INLAID CHAIR

FIG. 11.
QUEEN ANNE CHAIR

in France, our English style presents but few features in harmony with that of *Le Grand Monarque*. Still, it is well to remember that French influence was not wanting, nay, may have had more to do with the final determination of the style than many people imagine, for it is well known that the eminent designer, Daniel Marot, forced to leave Paris on the revocation of the Edict of Nantes, proceeded to Holland, where he received the ready patronage of William

13

of Orange. Further, it is chronicled that upon William ascending the English throne he appointed Marot as architect to the Crown. It is true there are no reliable records of work done by Marot in this country in the direction of architecture or furniture designing, though a plan for a garden is known inscribed, " *Parterre d'Amton-court, inventé par D.*

FIG. 12. QUEEN ANNE TABLE

Marot." Still, the presence of the great Frenchman is not to be ignored.

It is in this way that " styles " are usually formed. Many varying influences go to the making up of one mode. Sometimes a giant craftsman of strong personality and great gifts will stamp his name upon a particular order of designing, though even in such a case outside influences are invariably distinctly traceable. The man reaps a harvest sown by the unknown and often forgotten dead. But in most instances the creation of a style is the work of many; it is the blending of the best of many men's work; and this is true particularly of the style we call Queen Anne.

14

In one sense, the older designers had an advantage over their modern competitors, in that " novelties " were at once easier to introduce and more likely to meet " long-felt wants " than is the case after 200 years of activity in designing furniture to meet all requirements. In the older styles, such

FIG. 13. QUEEN ANNE CHAIR, IN WALNUT, EMBOSSED, PAINTED, AND GILT LEATHER (SOUTH KENSINGTON)

FIG. 14. QUEEN ANNE CHAIR

as the Queen Anne, we find many pieces introduced for the first time, at any rate in this country. Amongst the leading novelties of the Queen Anne style may be cited the " tall boy " chest of drawers; the Dutch corner cupboard; the bureau with elaborate interior fittings, secret drawers, etc.; and the now well-known high-backed chairs. Many other characteristic features of this style are presented in our various illustrations.

The tall boy chest is one of the best known features of the

Queen Anne style. The earlier examples display an amount of severity not subsequently maintained. Indeed, some of the later work in this style strongly indicates French influence, following more the lines of the Louis Quatorze chests than the severer Dutch designs. The typical Queen Anne chest has straight sides and an exceedingly simple pediment, and very little in the way of decoration beyond the metal

FIG. 15. QUEEN ANNE CHEST OF DRAWERS, PINE AND OAK, VENEERED LIGNUM-VITAE, WALNUT AND SYCAMORE

work used for handles, locks, etc. The C-shaped brass handles appear now for the first time, displacing the pear-shaped handles or dropped rings.

The bureau was sometimes replaced by a kind of secretaire without doors, but with numerous little drawers and pigeon holes, after the style of the modern American desk. Turned legs, sometimes quite elaborate in design, usually graced these articles.

Queen Anne chairs take many forms, but the most typical

16

are the Dutch chairs with cabriole legs, made in walnut or mahogany, the latter wood at this time commencing to become popular. The foot of the leg is "club," or, a later development, the ball and claw. Sometimes the legs are ornamented by a little carving, but generally they are plain. The fancy seems to have been for strong frames and high

FIG. 16. QUEEN ANNE CHAIR, IN WALNUT, COVERED WITH EMBROIDERED PETIT POINT, IN COLOURED WOOLS AND SILKS ON VELVET

FIG. 17. QUEEN ANNE CHAIR, STAINED, WITH PAINTED DECORATIONS

backs. The centre part of the back is often a flat splat, of severe outline. Some chairs of this period have upholstered seats and backs, whilst articles resembling the modern settee, or at any rate fulfilling a similar purpose, are to be found in the "double chairs," resembling two armchairs placed side by side, the inner arms being removed and the legs reduced to six in number. We illustrate a capital example of these articles. The later Queen Anne chairs are more ornate. The legs are often decorated with a kind of shell ornament and the splat is divided curiously, and sometimes relieved by carving. The three-cornered chair belongs to this period, also the chair with turned legs, a semicircular seat and a back rising to the height of about 4 ft. The great strength of most of the chairs of this date is proved by the

FIG. 18. QUEEN ANNE SETTEE

fact that many original pieces are still in everyday use, apparently but little the worse for their services during some two centuries.

Nearly all the typical chairs of the Queen Anne style will be found illustrated in our pages. The fine upholstered chair, covered in painted and gilt leather, is in the South Kensington Museum. Another excellent specimen is the armchair covered with embroidered *petit point* in coloured wools and silks on velvet, and a curious pattern is shown, with the shell ornament referred to above. This is a stained chair, with painted decoration.

We must not omit a reference to the celebrated clock

18

cases of this date. Some of the finest marquetery decorations are to be found here. Dutch cabinet-makers greatly favoured marquetery of a bold character, and the quality of their work varies very much, some of it being very beautiful, but a good deal of it quite the reverse.

Lovers of the Queen Anne style will experience some amount of difficulty in viewing choice specimens, as there

FIG. 19. TWO TYPICAL QUEEN ANNE CHAIRS

are few collections worth seeing available for public inspection. Perhaps the best place to go to for this purpose is the Hampton Court Palace, where a great deal of the furniture is in the style of this period. Apart from this fine collection, however, pieces of genuine Queen Anne furniture are, generally speaking, only to be found in isolated examples, though there are some very good specimens in the South Kensington Museum.

A feature not to be overlooked concerning the Queen Anne style is the enormous strides it accomplished in the direction of comfort. It has not always been recognized that comfort is an essential feature of good furniture, and the productions of this period may fairly be said to have laid the foundations of the modern comfortable home.

Of Grinling Gibbons it is unnecessary to say much. His fame rests upon his work, and he cannot be rated too highly.

FIG. 20. QUEEN ANNE TABLE

Some of his work, and perhaps some of the finest, is to be seen at Hampton Court Palace, round pictures, over the fireplaces, and on the mouldings of doorways. Flowers and fruit, beautifully grouped, are the subjects he preferred. Other specimens of his carving are to be found in St. Paul's Cathedral, in the choir stalls and side aisles. There is also a very fine doorway to be seen at the church of St. Nicholas Cole Abbey, Queen Victoria Street, E.C. Space forbids us mentioning, however, a tithe of the extant examples of the work of this great woodcarver.

We have referred to the fine work in the Queen Anne

20

style to be seen at the Hampton Court Palace, and it is
not inappropriate to remember the large part played by
William of Orange in the restoration of that royal residence.
Finding the air of London unsuitable to his poor health,
William made Hampton Court his headquarters, and highly

<table>
<tr><td>FIG. 21.
QUEEN ANNE CHAIR</td><td>FIG. 22.
QUEEN ANNE ARMCHAIR</td></tr>
</table>

interesting is the account of the fitting-up and furnishing
of the Palace under his direction. Macaulay says—

Much idle ingenuity was employed in forming that intricate labyrinth
of verdure which has puzzled and amused generations of holiday visitors
from London. . . . A new court, not designed with the purest taste, but
stately, spacious and commodious, rose under the direction of Wren. The
wainscots were adorned with the rich and delicate carvings of Gibbons.
The staircases were in a blaze with the glaring frescoes of Verris. In every
corner of the mansion appeared a profusion of gew-gaws, not yet familiar
to English eyes. Mary had acquired at The Hague a taste for the porcelain

of China, and amused herself by forming at Hampton a vast collection of hideous images, and of vases on which houses, trees, bridges and mandarins were depicted in outrageous defiance of all the laws of perspective. The fashion, a frivolous and inelegant fashion, it must be owned, which was thus set by the amiable Queen, spread fast and wide. In a few years almost every great house in the Kingdom contained a museum of these grotesque baubles. . . . Satirists long continued to repeat that a fine lady valued her mottled green pottery quite as much as she valued her monkey, and much more than she valued her husband.

FIG. 23. QUEEN ANNE CHAIR

It is worth noting, in passing, that during the reign of Queen Anne the influence of French craftsmen was increasingly felt. Some seventeen years before she came to the throne (in the reign of James II) Louis XIV in his Catholic zeal had revoked the Edict of Nantes, and large numbers of French Protestants took refuge in this country. The refugees were industrious, thrifty, and upright, and undoubtedly did much in the direction of shaping certain industries in this country. The case of the Spitalfields weavers, though a prominent instance, is not an isolated one. The Huguenots

22

FIG. 24. QUEEN ANNE SETTEE

FIG. 25. QUEEN ANNE CHAIR   FIG. 26. QUEEN ANNE CHAIR

23

were not in any sense of the term " undesirable aliens," and as in the reign of Anne they had had time to settle down their presence counts for much. This subject is one of great interest, but we cannot here give to it more than a passing allusion.

The period under consideration has bequeathed to us the names of no great individual furniture designers, but its influence may be said to have coloured a good deal of the work done during the eighteenth century, as the student of Chippendale furniture will quickly recognize. As to the future, anything in the nature of a revival of the Queen Anne style is hardly to be expected, not because that mode did not contain some imperishable phases, but rather because all that was best in it was taken up and absorbed by later expressions, and improved in that evolutionary process. Therefore, though some Queen Anne pieces still retain a measure of popularity, and enthusiasts are not wanting to sing the praises of the mode, speaking generally we may safely conclude that the work of the style is done. It died in giving birth to something nobler and more artistic.

CHAPTER III

THE LOUIS XIV STYLE

NOMINALLY the reign of Louis Quatorze covers the whole of the latter half of the seventeenth century and the first fifteen years of the eighteenth; but, of course, Louis himself was but 5 years old when his father died and left him heir to the throne of France. With the political aspect of his reign we are not concerned, save only to note that at this time France was the dominant power in Europe and the wealthiest of European powers. That fact being borne in mind will tend to explain the development of the Louis XIV style, which is contemporaneous with our William and Mary and Queen Anne styles.

It would be interesting to trace the earlier stages of French decorative art, but that would be too big a task in a volume of this size. We may say, however, that in commencing our French styles with Louis XIV, the period of the later Renaissance, we include all that is of real modern significance; and fascinating as is the study of the earlier times, it is of little importance from a practical point of view. By the middle of the seventeenth century the French Renaissance had separated itself from its early Italian forms, and had taken distinctive lines of its own. Comfort had become a consideration, and furniture was being constructed from that point of view. Thus was the way prepared for the *Grand Monarque*, who in 1643 became King of France.

Like all general denominations, Louis Quatorze denotes a mixture of many influences—Italian, Flemish, and French. Under the direction of Richelieu, modern Italian work was largely popularized, whilst the King was a liberal patron of

25

handicrafts, continuing the work of State patronage commenced by Henri IV, who established the Louvre for the

FIG. 27. LOUIS XIV DETAILS

encouragement of industrial art. Not only was native talent developed, but considerable patronage was extended to foreign workmen, who were given a ready welcome, and to this must be attributed much of the early greatness of France in this direction. The furniture produced included cabinets in cedar, or marquetery, and ebony inlaid with ivory or metal,

FIG. 28. LOUIS XIV DETAILS

sometimes decorated with coloured marble. Both straight and curved legs were in vogue. The decorations were largely in the form of allegorical figures and geometric designs.

27

Flowers and fruit, too, are prominent and take shapes more natural than in the earlier forms. Carved and gilt wood was freely used.

The extravagance of Louis XIV is well known, though it is exceedingly doubtful whether any of the usual estimates concerning his expenditure are reliable. Some authorities put it at ten million sterling per annum. Certainly his monumental work in the Palace of Versailles must have necessitated enormous sums of money being spent, and a great impetus was given to the furniture industry. The foundation of the Gobelins' factory must be dealt with separately later in this chapter.

Naturally, at Versailles are to be found some of the greatest achievements of the period. To attempt anything like a description of them would demand a separate volume. One apartment, the Œil de Bœuf, has been immortalized by Thomas Carlyle, in his *French Revolution*, as being the meeting-place of the Court of the unhappy Louis XVI.

Among the most celebrated artists and designers of the time were André Charles Boulle, Charles Le Brun, Jean Berain, Jean Le Pautre, and Daniel Marot, though many other names might be added. The two first-named we deal with later in this chapter. Berain was a talented designer and, with Marot, was employed by the great Boulle. Let the visitor to Versailles who desires to see something of what the artists of this period could do, view the Galerie des Glaces, the Salon de l'Abondance, the Salon d'Apollon, the royal bedchambers, or the Salon de la Guerre—and these are but examples. Of course, later expressions are now also to be found at Versailles, e.g. Louis XV and Louis XVI. Our illustration will convey a general idea of the leading characteristics of this period. In this country some excellent pieces of the style may be seen in the Wallace Collection, and at South Kensington are a few more. A few years ago a set of

28

six Louis XIV chairs, in Gobelins' tapestry, fetched the extraordinary sum of £20,000. That, of course, is quite a

FIG. 29. LOUIS XIV DETAILS

fictitious value, but good prices have frequently been made for fine examples of the period.

André Charles Boulle, whose name has been given to the particular kind of work he originated (generally written

Buhl work), was attached to the Royal Furniture Factory of the Gobelins. Strange irony of fate it seems that so great a genius should have ended his days in the direst poverty, being reduced even to the adoption of the most shady tactics to obtain the money he needed. His misfortunes were in part attributable to the act of an incendiary who burnt down

FIG. 30. LOUIS XIV CHAIR

Boulle's workshops and warehouses, in which were contained a valuable collection of artistic treasures. Of this fire, Boulle wrote—

All that could be done was to bear away the few things closest to hand, leaving all else to be destroyed.

He died at a ripe old age, in great poverty, having exhausted the patience of all his patrons and suffered every indignity of the insolvent.

Yet some of his productions are ranked with the world's

30

masterpieces. The feature of his work (continued after his death by his sons) was not in that he invented any new

FIG. 31. AN ARMOIRE, BY ANDRÉ CHARLES BOULLE

process, but rather that he brought to perfection an older one. The use of tortoiseshell and copper for decorating ebony cabinets may be traced back to a date long before Boulle was born. The "Boulle" marquetery method was

31

to glue together two or three thicknesses of copper, ebony, and tortoiseshell. These were sawn through to the necessary pattern.

When the sheets are detached one has in hand, should copper and inlaying tortoiseshell have been employed, two decorative patterns and two grounds for inlaying—that is to say, the sheets of shell or copper out of which the patterns have been cut. The next step is to insert the copper pattern in the shell ground, and the shell pattern in the copper ground. Two panels are thus obtained, totally different in aspect, but absolutely alike in pattern. (Molinier, quoted by Lady Dilke.)

These parts are termed the " boulle " and " counter." Some very fine specimens of Boulle's work are still extant, but, being very perishable, cannot, of course, be seen in their perfection. Some imitations, however, rival the work of Boulle himself, and even experts have been deceived by them.

The tremendous work of completing the Palace at Versailles naturally opened up great opportunities for the furniture makers. Even in its present form, when whole suites of apartments have been destroyed in the process of turning them into galleries, some idea of the gigantic enterprise may be formed. It is not too much to say that the richness of the treasure there palls upon the casual visitor as he walks through the galleries and apartments. What must such a work have meant to the furniture makers of the time? The curious may still inspect the originals of some of the contracts given out by Louis XIV.

The Gobelins' factory derives its name from a Flemish family, its founders, and was purchased by Louis XIV. It became a furniture factory as well as a tapestry factory, and the splendid fabric representing a visit paid by Louis to the premises, shows that monarch inspecting cabinets and other pieces of furniture. Charles Le Brun, the then director, was a great designer, and to him, in large measure, belongs the credit of the Gobelins' greatness. Naturally, in a volume

32

FIG. 32. LOUIS XIV CABINET

of this size, it is only possible to mention this establishment. A larger work than this could be filled with a description of some of its historic productions.

Gobelins' tapestry is unique, and many of the finest pieces produced during this reign may be inspected. The series, " Histoire de Roi," " The King entering Dunkerque," " L'incendie du bourg de Rome," " Héliodore chassé du Temple," and the series including the " Triomphe de Bacchus," " Triomphe de Mars," and " Triomphe de la Philosophie," may be mentioned as typical expressions of the *tapissier's* art under Louis XIV. Another fine series of panels executed in this reign represented scenes taken from the Old Testament.

Louis XIV designs can only be properly reproduced at considerable expense. The style is not suitable for cheap representation. Economy was not one of the virtues of Louis Quatorze.

CHAPTER IV

THE LOUIS XV STYLE

THE close connection invariably to be traced between the history of a country and its expressions of industrial art is perhaps more distinct in the style called Louis Quinze than in any other. The magnificence and ostentatious

FIG. 33. LOUIS XV CHAIR   FIG. 34. LOUIS XV CHAIR

extravagance of the preceding reign developed naturally into the rococo of Louis XV.

The Louis Quinze period may be divided into two parts, viz. the Regency and the Rococo, the first covering a period of eight years, during which time (Louis XV being only 5 years old on the death of his great-grandfather, Louis XIV) Philip, Duc d'Orleans, was Regent. On Philip's death, in 1723, the King was proclaimed as " of age," he being then 13.

Some familiarity with French history is absolutely necessary to the proper understanding of the French styles. During *l'époque de la Régence* the social conditions in France were undergoing great changes. The huge demands made upon the nation by the reckless extravagance of Louis XIV had sown a harvest which was rapidly ripening and was to have terrible results. At this time financial embarrassment was the condition of the Court and the *noblesse*, and it became practically impossible to continue the great receptions and entertainments customary in the reign of Louis the Magnificent. The influence of this state of affairs on the

FIG. 35. MODERN LOUIS XV SETTEE

furniture designers was immediate in its effect. As one writer, describing the period, has put it—

The boudoir became of more importance than the salon. Instead of the majestic grandeur of immense reception rooms and stately galleries, were the elegance and prettiness of the boudoir.

There, in brief, is an indication of the change taking place in the furniture styles. As the period developed, ornament became richer and richer. Rooms were freely decorated—over-decorated would be the modern opinion. Cupids, heads and female busts, fountains, flowers, shells, doves, etc., carved or moulded, adorned the windows, doors, and mirror frames. The furniture, too, was decorated to harmonize with this. The pieces became smaller altogether, as befitted

36

the new conditions, the frames in gilt, upholstered in Gobelins, Aubusson, or Beauvais tapestries. Inlays of marquetery

FIG. 36

and mother-o'-pearl are features of the period, whilst graceful curves take the place of the departing stately lines.

Shortly, the distinguishing features of the Louis Quinze
style may be summed up as follows: Smaller pieces, rococo
ornamentation, and delicate and graceful curved lines. The

37

tendency was in the direction of the effeminate—a feature writ large in every line of the history of this period.

Amongst the principal designers of this time (omitting Riesener and David Roentgen, dealt with under Louis XVI) were Nicholas Pineau, Jacques Caffieri, Jules-Aurèle Meissonnier, Jacques Blondel, Denizol, Charles Cressent, Jean Oeben, and the Martin family. Vernis-Martin (often incorrectly quoted as the name of a craftsman) is the title given

Fig. 37. Louis XV Settee

to the work of William Martin, originally a coach painter, the word *vernis*, meaning varnish or polish, being coupled with the surname Martin to denominate the particular work he did. Vernis-Martin panels form one of the most beautiful expressions of Louis Quinze decoration. Some splendid specimens of this work (as indeed of all the works of this period) are to be seen in the Wallace Collection. Perhaps there is no finer collection of French furniture in the world than this one, and its accessibility to English students renders it particularly valuable.

It would be inaccurate to convey the impression that the Louis Quinze style did not present much that was exceedingly beautiful. Unfortunately, it is the worst features that

38

are generally most prominent. The finest specimens, however, of the Pompadour style are marked by a freshness and
fascinating elegance unequalled, perhaps, anywhere. It may

FIG. 38. LOUIS XV COMMODE

also be noted that in reproducing this style, the costliness
practically prohibits the preservation of the finest features.
The work of Riesener or Boulle, or, indeed, of many of the
French *ébénists* of the period, cannot be repeated cheaply.

When every line in the cabinet work swells itself to assume fantastic
curves, when nothing is straight and regular, when everything is *bombé*

39

and twisted, and caricatured lines abound everywhere, when gilded and chased brass is needed at every corner, and when marble slabs and Sèvres panels are absolutely indispensable, how is it possible to make Louis Quinze cabinet work cheaply?

The Regency furniture reflects the best features of Louis Quatorze, but was considered " too heavy " for the day of Madame de Pompadour and Madame du Barry, and hence

FIG. 39. LOUIS XV SETTEE

the rapid disappearance of some of its most stately lines, the absence of which is one of the distinguishing features of the later period.

As stated above, Riesener and Roentgen, though at work during this reign, are usually reckoned as belonging to the Louis XVI epoch, and will be dealt with in that chapter. Mention must be made, however, of the celebrated *Bureau de Roi*, perhaps the most exquisite piece of Louis Quinze design produced. This magnificent article was the joint work of Oeben and Riesener. On it, in bronze gilt, are the figures of Calliope and Apollo, and toward the centre of the panel cupids are depicted, surrounding a medallion with the head of Minerva. The bureau is now in the Louvre.

FIG. 40. LOUIS XV ROCOCO DECORATION

Typical decoration in this style includes love tokens of all varieties, such as the cupid's bow, the lovers' knot, and so on. These details were later to become unrecognizable, lost

41

in scrolls and curves, definite outline apparently being forsaken in favour of rococo detail.

Characteristic pieces of the period that may be mentioned are the *bonheur de joir*, a small cabinet set on a table; the

FIG. 41. LOUIS XV THREE-FOLD SCREEN

étagère, or decorative hanging cabinet; the *encoignure*, or corner cabinet; occasional tables and threefold screens, the folds being of different height. The great popularity of lacquered panels, which process was probably invented by the Chinese, led to the native cultivation of the art. It is safe to assert, however, that the Chinese work was superior to the French. In many ways Chinese influence is apparent at this time, and it will be remembered that Chippendale,

42

in our own country, designed several distinctly Chinese pieces. In France, great freedom (to say the least) was exercised in adapting the ideas from the Far East.

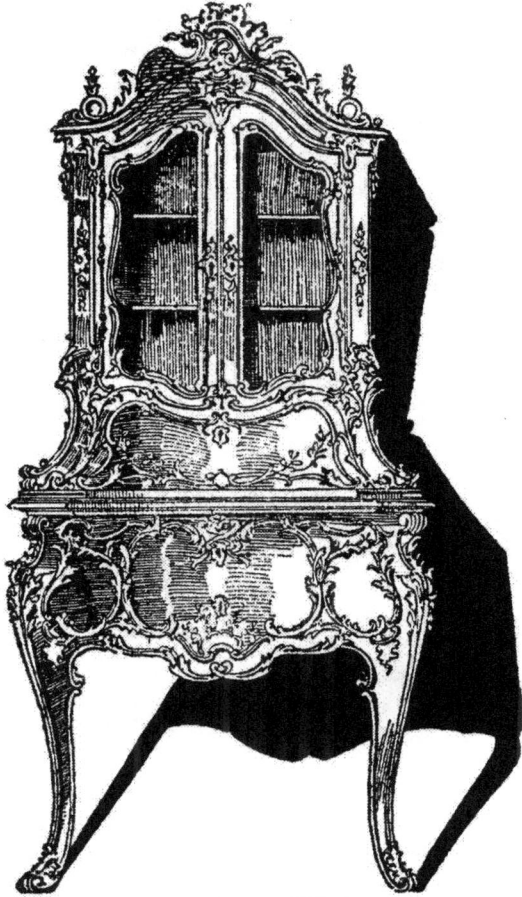

FIG. 42. LOUIS XV CABINET

It may be well to state here that the term *rococo* (lit. bad taste) and *rocaille* (lit. rock-work, rugged) are used to represent practically the same thing, viz. the excessive ornamentation and extravagance of the designs of this period, and the

43

use of ornate decoration without reference to the appropriateness of its employment. Louis Quinze furniture has been briefly described as the " triumph of curves," and, perhaps, in a nutshell, that denotes with a fair degree of accuracy the distinguisning feature of the style. Yet, in economical reproductions, that is the very feature generally minimized—on the score of expense, of course.

Experts say that during the reign of Louis XV no less than eight distinct furniture styles are traceable. It will consequently be understood that we are able to deal only with general characteristics.

CHAPTER V

THE CHIPPENDALE STYLE

UNLIKE many of the great masters of furniture designing and manufacture, the life-story of Thomas Chippendale has no pathetic note. Though history does not tell us very much concerning the details of his life, it reveals to us, beyond much doubt, that Chippendale was not by any means allowed to give his treasures to the world unrewarded except by that satisfaction which is only known to the craftsman who has done good work. On the contrary, there are not wanting indications that Chippendale's genius was recognized before it was too late for him to profit by such recognition; and though, indeed, no such fabulous figures were paid for his productions as those at which they have since changed hands, he reaped a sufficiently rich harvest to spend his days in comfort and in the enjoyment of quite a moderate share of the world's pleasures.

Thomas Chippendale was born in the first half of the eighteenth century. The year and the place of his birth are both unknown. He came of a Worcester family of carvers, and his early training, therefore, may be taken to have been a practical introduction to the work of his life.

His father seems to have settled in London and traded as a cabinet-maker in St. Martin's Lane, an aristocratic neighbourhood at that time. Here the great designer worked and turned out his masterpieces, conscious, no doubt, that his work was good and valuable, but how little could he have recognized the true greatness of what he did! He has since become the author of one of the most popular styles—the creator of many of the most costly pieces of furniture in existence.

45

Of his life but little more is known. His personal character can only be revealed to us by his works, yet if John Ruskin has taught us a true theory, may we not unhesitatingly attribute to Chippendale that honesty which covers and colours the whole life? It is only the true work that lives; untrue work may have its day, but the test of time banishes

FIG. 43. CHIPPENDALE CHAIR

all save the true. Judged by such a standard, Thomas Chippendale should occupy an exalted position indeed.

Chippendale's book was published in 1754. A second edition followed five years later, and a third in 1762. The title according to the title page was *The Gentleman and Cabinetmaker's Director : Being a large collection of the most elegant and useful designs of household furniture in the most fashionable taste.* Then follows a long list of articles included in the volume, and the title page goes on to say—

To which is prefixed a short explanation of the five orders of architecture, with proper directions for executing the most difficult pieces, the

46

mouldings being exhibited at large, and the dimensions of each design specified. The whole comprehended in two hundred copper plates, neatly engraved. Calculated to improve and refine the present taste, and suited to the fancy and circumstances of persons in all degrees of life. By Thomas Chippendale, Cabinet-maker and Upholsterer in St. Martin's Lane, London.

The following paragraph also appears—

The title page has already called the following work, *The Gentleman and Cabinetmaker's Director*, as being calculated to assist the one in the

FIG. 44. CHIPPENDALE SETTEE

choice and the other in the execution of the designs; which are so contrived that if no one drawing should singly answer the gentleman's taste, there will yet be found a variety of hints, sufficient to construct a new one.

In the light of subsequent developments, the delightful egotism displayed in the wording of the title page is overlooked. Or is it, after all, the consciousness of a master which inspires the language?

With regard to the " Five Orders of Architecture " referred to, we may dismiss this portion of Chippendale's book with the remark that it was not unusual for eighteenth-century writers on furniture to give such treatises. It will be remembered that Sheraton followed the practice in his *Cabinet-maker and Upholsterer's Drawing Book*. It was in this volume, too, that Sheraton gave us his estimate of the work

FIG. 45. CHIPPENDALE CHAIR

of his great predecessor. Speaking of Chippendale's productions, he says—

They are now wholly antiquated and laid aside, though possessed of great merit, according to the times in which they were executed.

But Sheraton's verdict has been totally upset. Chippendale is not out of date yet, nor is there any sign that his popularity is on the wane.

The style of Chippendale, of course, varies considerably. It is said sometimes that " fashions all come from Paris." Be that as it may, unquestionably much of Chippendale's earlier work was influenced, if not actually directed, by the

48

French styles, particularly Louis XIV and Louis XV, the latter of which may be said to be the inspiring source of the

FIG. 46. CHIPPENDALE CABINET

cabriole leg. Many people appear to think that the cabriole leg may be accepted as a sure sign of Chippendale's work, but this is not correct, and many of his finest productions

4—(6185)

have square legs. In many of his chair backs, too, Chippendale has followed the French styles. Whilst not above adopting prevailing French fashions to meet the requirements of his patrons, it may be said in Chippendale's defence that he always strove to introduce an original idea, even where the foundation was obviously borrowed. This is apparent in the

FIG. 47. FRENCH CHIPPENDALE CHAIR (EARLY)

ribbon-back chairs, where the Louis design is twisted and modified into an English pattern.

Chippendale was also considerably influenced by Chinese designs. To a great measure this may be attributed to the work of Sir William Chambers, a remarkable man, about whom a few lines may not be out of place, considering how largely he influenced Chippendale's work. Sir William Chambers it was who designed and laid out Kew Gardens, and
50

built the famous pagoda there. As a boy his inclinations were for travel, and he seems to have become possessed with the beauty of Chinese buildings and art productions. He was in the habit of making rough sketches of things that caught his fancy, and these, on his return, were drawn by

FIG. 48. FRENCH CHIPPENDALE CHAIR (EARLY)

capable artists and published in 1757, and a second batch followed in 1765. Subsequently his Chinese enthusiasm led him into some amount of disrepute, but he regained his reputation by his work as architect of Somerset House, and he rests in Westminster Abbey. It is clear that Chippendale must have had access to Sir William's Chinese designs, or many of them, as, although they were not published until three years after the appearance of *The Gentleman and Cabinetmaker's Director*, their influence is clearly to be traced

51

in many of the illustrations in that great work. Not that Chippendale adopted the Chinese designs by slavishly copying what he saw. As a genius he recognized an opportunity. He saw in this particular kind of detail a fine opening for new designs, and we may say pretty confidently that much

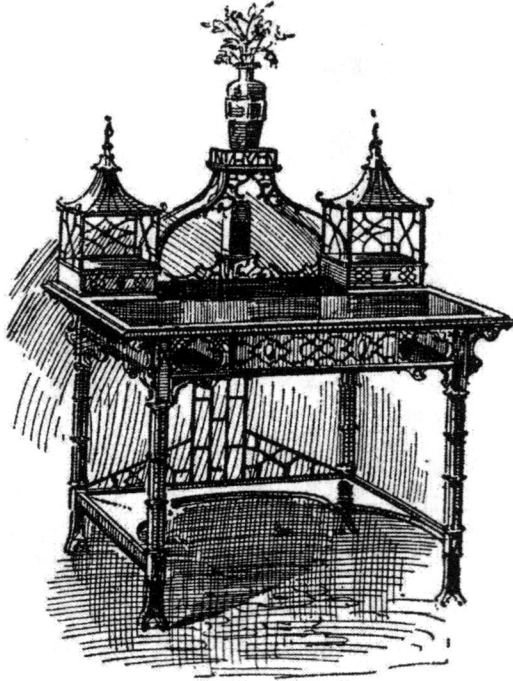

FIG. 49. CHINESE CHIPPENDALE WRITING TABLE

of the Chinese-like fretwork in the backs of his chairs, on the face of chair-legs, and elsewhere, had its real origin no further east than St. Martin's Lane. The Chinese influence also appears in much of Chippendale's ornament. In his looking-glasses in this style we come across pagoda-like pinnacles and other embellishments from the Far East.

The Gothic also influenced one period of Chippendale's

52

productions, as there occurred a temporary revival of this
style. The real strength and beauty of Chippendale is not,
however, French, Chinese, or Gothic, but rather is a combination of all three, blended and harmonized by the touch
of a master hand. And of such transcendent importance is
that " touch," that it creates for us an original style, having
new beauties of its own, belonging to none of the sources of
its inspiration. That is where the great designer's power

FIG. 50. CHIPPENDALE SETTEE

was—in his ability to use foreign influences in the production of a new English style.

Nearly all of Chippendale's work was in mahogany, without any inlaying. He used brass mounts and sometimes
silver and copper. Some of his productions were in rosewood. Great strength is a feature of his chairs, as he took
great pains to make them durable, by fixing the chair splat
into the frames, a practice which has not always been followed by subsequent makers.

Among Chippendale's contemporaries there were not

lacking those who hesitated not to scoff at his Chinese and Gothic designs as impracticable. He answers them in his Preface—

I have here given no design but what may be executed with advantage by the hands of a skilful workman, though some of the profession (*sic*) have been diligent enough to represent them (especially those after the Gothic and Chinese manner) as so many specious drawings, impossible to be worked off by any mechanic whatsoever. I will not scruple to attribute this to malice, ignorance and inability; and I am confident I can convince all noblemen, gentlemen and others, who will honour me with their commands, that every design in the book can be improved in the execution of it, by their most obedient servant, Thomas Chippendale.

Cabinet-making was a "profession" to Chippendale. There is a lesson in his use of the word.

Chippendale foresaw criticism. Indeed, he writes as though he had already experienced it.

I am not afraid (he says) of the fate an author usually meets with on his first appearance, from a set of critics who are never wanting to show their wit and malice on the performances of others: I shall repay their censures with contempt. Let them unmolested deal out their pointless abuse, and convince the world they have neither good nature to commend, judgment to correct nor skill to execute what they find fault with.

Poor old Chippendale! Like many a one before and since he, unmindful of the greatness of his work, concerns and frets himself with the " troublesome insects of the hour," as Carlyle has it. Could he but return to his familiar haunts to-day, he would with emphasis agree that wisdom is justified of her children.

His furniture has realized enormous prices in recent times, and its vogue among collectors shows no sign of decline.

The illustrations accompanying this chapter may be accepted as generally representative of the Chippendale style —a style, be it said, that is not likely to decrease in popularity for a long time to come.

It is in Chippendale's furniture that we first find anything like full advantage taken of the properties of mahogany, though he did not, like Heppelwhite, carry lightness to the

FIG. 51. CHIPPENDALE CABINET

extreme limits of safety. For a long time it was without a rival, but when satinwood, tulipwood, and other fancy woods came into vogue, Heppelwhite slightingly mentions it as

55

one of the " inferior woods " in which certain designs may, for cheapness, be carried out.

It is interesting, in passing, to note that the Preface to Chippendale's book, worded in pompous and grandiose language, was not his own unaided production. When one learns that Dr. Johnson had a hand in its composition, the grandiloquent expressions are at once explained.

Certain it is, if Boswell may be trusted, that the Chinese designs of Sir William Chambers found an enthusiastic admirer in Dr. Johnson, who said of Sir William's book: " It wants no addition nor correction, but a few lines of introduction," which the good Doctor furnished and Sir William adopted. Was his service to Chippendale less ready? We fancy not, and it opens up a fascinating vista of thought as to the possible relations of the two masters in widely different walks of life.

CHAPTER VI

THE SHERATON STYLE

It is perhaps not too much to say that Sheraton has given us the most beautiful furniture of all the designers, and his graceful outlines will always secure for him a grateful memory with lovers of art furniture.

Thomas Sheraton was a Durham man, coming from Stock-

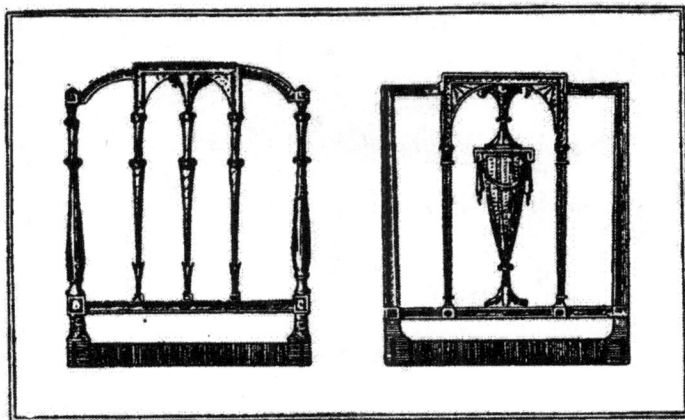

FIG. 52. SHERATON CHAIR BACKS

ton-on-Tees, at which place he was born in 1751. Of education, as we understand it, he had practically none, though, inasmuch as his parents intended that he should follow the profession of an architect, he naturally gave some attention to drawing. It is undoubtedly due to this cause that a large proportion of his decorative designs should have been carefully drawn to scale, like architectural plans. Circumstances, however, led to his turning from architecture to the designing of furniture, and the world has benefited thereby, for, though it is not possible to say how far Sheraton would have

57

succeeded in taking rank with the great names in building construction, it is not likely that he would have risen to the eminence that he has achieved in the industry he selected. It is probably one of those cases where the particular talent

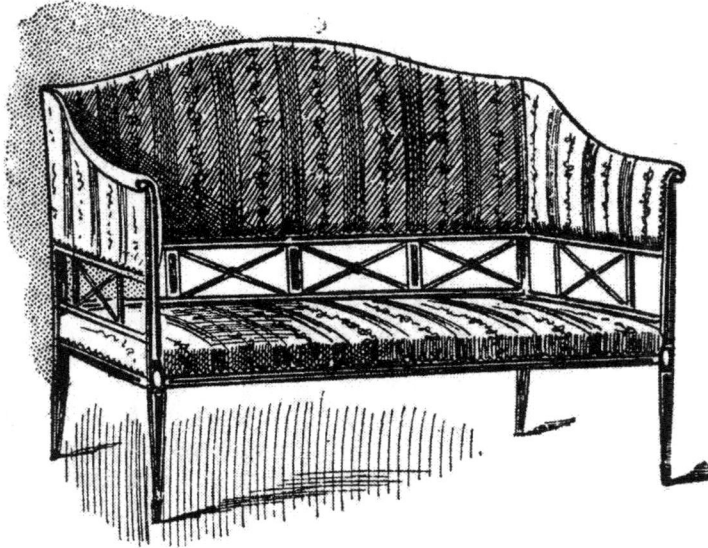

FIG. 53. SHERATON SETTEE

of the man will find its natural bent, proving, as it has been proved over and over again, that—

> There's a divinity that shapes our ends,
> Rough-hew them how we will.

The life-story of Sheraton is simple and pathetic. It is a real life tragedy of unrecognized, or at least unrewarded, genius. Like many another of the world's great masters in science, literature, and art, he presented creations almost priceless, and received in return the means of the barest existence. The story of this honest eighteenth-century craftsman toiling at his work with the determination and doggedness of one who knows the worth of what he is doing,

58

and earning hardly sufficient to support himself and his family, is one of those sad pages which abound in history.

FIG. 54. CABINET IN THE SHERATON STYLE

His reward was in the future. If Sheraton could live to-day he would feel that his anxious years of labour had been fully justified.

As a matter of fact, during his life Sheraton never received

59

ample remuneration for any of his works. He published altogether five books. The first is called *The Cabinetmaker and Upholsterer's Drawing Book,* in which he gave instructions on the art of making perspective drawings. In it he also gave " Five Orders " for cabinet-makers. His references to Chippendale sound strangely in our ears, who have learned

FIG. 55. SHERATON WRITING TABLE

to regard that designer as one of the great, and whose furniture has of late years fetched such extraordinary prices at auction sales. Sheraton speaks of Chippendale's productions as " now wholly antiquated and laid aside, though possessed of great merit, according to the times in which they were executed." Seeing that but a quarter of a century divided

the two designers, this brings into prominence the truth
that it is difficult to form a proportionate estimate where no

FIG. 56. SHERATON CABINET

long period of time has pronounced the more infallible judgment. In these matters time tells the truth, as the often
unjust, though honest, opinion of the contemporaries of a
genius reveals to the men of a later date.

Sheraton divided this book into four parts. The first provides the workman with that geometrical teaching which the author had learned in his early days to value. The second part deals with perspective; the third provides furniture designs; whilst the fourth deals with decorative designs,

FIG. 57. SHERATON CHAIR

mouldings, and ornaments. Not a little of the permanence and value of the work is due to the extreme care which the author took to make his explanations, especially those difficult in the very nature of the subject, perfectly clear.

In 1803 Sheraton published *The Cabinet Dictionary*, and a few years later *The Cabinetmaker, Upholsterer and General Artist's Encyclopædia*. These volumes, of which the first-named was illustrated with coloured plates, deal with

62

designs of chairs and furniture generally. The artist is evidenced by a brief quotation from the former book. Sheraton

FIG. 58. SHERATON CHINA CABINET

is speaking of the remarkable fact that there is often a difference in chairs of precisely the same pattern when executed by different chairmakers, and he explains this by the

63

suggestion that it arises chiefly from the want of taste concerning the beauty of an outline, " of which we judge by the eye, more than the rigid rules of geometry."

It lends an additional note of pathos to the history of this great designer to learn that throughout his entire life he continued a devoutly religious man. He was a Baptist and

FIG. 59. SHERATON CHAIR

wrote several treatises on religious subjects. His lack of monetary success was not attributable to any personal extravagance or want of industry. Yet his works brought him but poor reward, and when he died, in 1806, after having been in London for some sixteen years, he left his family quite unprovided for. Striking indeed is the contrast when we turn to the records of sale prices of Sheraton's productions. On the one hand the maker dies in neglected poverty,

64

on the other his designs make rich those who come after.
A toilet table of satinwood, bought for the South Kensington

FIG. 60. CABINET IN THE SHERATON STYLE

Museum, cost the authorities £200; whilst a miniature cabinet at £52, a satinwood cabinet at £200, and a semi-oval
form table at £78 15s., have also been added to the collection

of our national woodwork. At auction a satinwood secretaire bookcase sold for £173, a satinwood cabinet for
£250, another for £141, six satinwood chairs for £105, and
a suite for £400. Would not such sums have rejoiced the

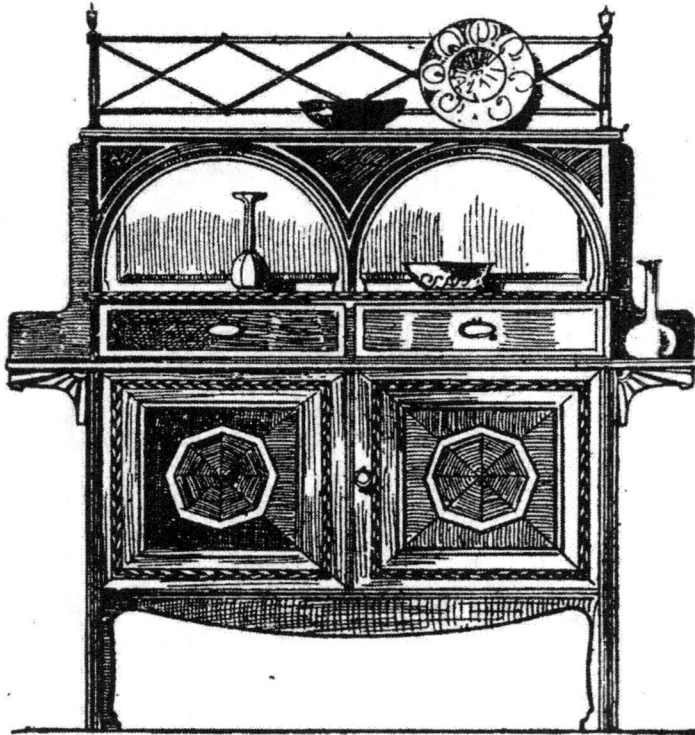

FIG. 61. SHERATON SIDEBOARD

heart of their maker! But it is the law of all life—one
sows, another reaps.

The ruling ideas of Sheraton's designs are simplicity and
usefulness. He sought to combine what was best in the
Louis XVI style with a total—or almost so—repression of
ornate decoration. Until quite modern times his masterpieces remained unappreciated, but are now admitted to the
66

highest place among the best expressions of the cabinet-maker's art.

As a specimen of Sheraton's descriptive care, we quote his

FIG. 62. SHERATON SIDEBOARD

remarks about one of his designs for ornamenting a painted panel. He says—

The whole springs from a spreading leaf at the bottom, from which a serpent attempts to come at the doves on the fruit. In the centre is a temple not dedicated to the interests of the cupids, for which reason they are burning it with their torches. The figure on the top of the column, in

67

resenting it, means to pelt them with stones and the geniuses above are pouring down water to quench the flames. The owls are emblematic of Night, at which season these mischiefs are generally carried on.

FIG. 63. SHERATON SIDEBOARD

From such a description one could almost reproduce the panel.

Our illustrations need no comment. They are given as illustrative generally of the style of this great designer.

It is interesting that Sheraton's earliest productions were refined and spontaneous in spirit—maybe that hope was

68

brightest then. His later works are more laboured, though still beautiful, for, despite disappointment, and amid environments less lovely than his thoughts, his life was consistently pure, though his habits were undoubtedly eccentric.

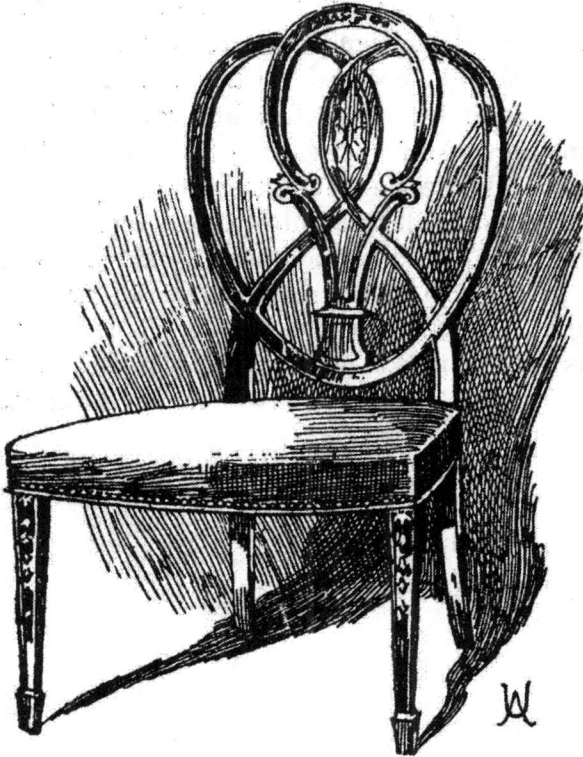

FIG. 64. SHERATON CHAIR

Toward the end of his career his individuality seems to have weakened—and whose would not under such neglect? Instead of quietly pursuing his own innate fancies, and endeavouring thereby to educate public taste toward refinement, his former so persistent originality now began to shrink, and gradually, in the absence of incentive from within, the labours of the great designer began to reflect the

69

hard fashions that were growing up around him. Sheraton's style is, with one exception, the only truly national and nature-born style of art of which the furniture man can boast. Yet, at the time of its inception, so indifferent were we to its charms that we allowed its creator to die in want, and even to desert his own invention ere he departed. The English style that he created, he himself forsook in his last few years—for his latest productions were designed in listless agreement with the prevailing fashions which servilely copied the pseudo-classic art of our hereditary enemies across the channel. You will remember that we were at war with France when Sheraton was approaching the end of his career. Yet here was a creator of a patriotic style, driven, through sheer disgust at the neglect his people dealt out to him, to forsake his native style and pander to the Empire style that Caesarism, under Napoleon, was fast making *de rigueur* among our then bellicose rivals.

CHAPTER VII

THE ADAM STYLE

IN a village near Kirkcaldy lived William Adam, an architect of considerable local fame. His practice was an extensive one, and he held the office of Master Mason of Scotland, and was the architect of some famous buildings in that country, including Hopetoun House. He had four sons—John, James, William, and Robert. John followed and inherited his father's business; William, it is probable, assisted his brothers; and it is with Robert and James that this chapter is concerned, for to them is due the credit of initiating the style bearing their name.

Robert Adam was born in 1728, and was the second son. His was the master mind—the dominating spirit. A contemporary of Sir William Chambers, there was much in common between the two men, although perhaps Robert Adam never attained to the intellectual stature of Sir William. Robert Adam caught the spirit of his age, which was a spirit of restlessness and of inquiry after something better in art. The cynics say that mere change—the finding of " something new "—was the popular desire; but the student, who is not content with a surface view of the facts, diving a little deeper, finds evidence of a real and earnest effort to achieve something higher. It was this that drove Robert Adam, as it drove many another, to travel. He visited Italy when he was about 28 years of age, and made a close study of all that was there, including the remains of Emperor Diocletian's Palace at Spalatro; and the companionship of Clérisseau, the eminent French architect, was, no doubt, of material use to him in many ways. He was also, probably, influenced to a considerable extent by other French artists, and some

71

Adam work shows unmistakable signs of this, and has even been humorously called " an English edition of the Louis Seize style."

His foreign studies lasted some few years, and it was not until 1762 that he returned from Italy, when he was appointed by George III as his architect. He died in 1792,

FIG. 65. OCCASIONAL TABLE AND CHAIR IN THE ADAM STYLE

as the result of a broken blood vessel, and is buried in Westminster Abbey.

Of James Adam but little is known beyond his connection with his illustrious brother, whom he outlived but two years. That he had invaluable qualities we may assume from the long partnership between Robert and himself, but beyond what may be deduced from this, James Adam is practically an unknown quantity. That Robert was the moving spirit of the partnership is certain. May we not fairly conclude

72

that whilst Robert supplied the brilliancy, the genius and the initiative, James brought to the work the steadiness, the painstaking care, and the constant application, for lack of which sound qualities genius is so often dissipated? It is a

FIG. 66. BOUDOIR WRITING TABLE IN THE ADAM STYLE

guess, but it is a hazard in defence of which much might be written. In any event, it does injustice to neither brother, and probably appraises with a great degree of accuracy the particular virtues of both. So much for the personal side. What of their work?

Primarily architects, the brothers Adam seem to have devoted themselves to furniture designing in order that

73

the furniture in some of the exquisite apartments they were responsible for should be in entire harmony with its surroundings. In general terms, the Adam style may be described as an adaptation or development (whichever is preferred) of the pure Classic of Greece and Italy, modified

FIG. 67. SIDEBOARD IN THE ADAM STYLE

occasionally by French ideas, such, for instance, as the gilding of furniture. Another feature of Adam furniture was the application of composition ornaments to woodwork. Festoons of drapery or wreaths of flowers, caught up with a ram's head or tied with a knot of ribbon, are characteristic ornaments of the style. Their furniture was manufactured chiefly in mahogany, carved, and sometimes inlaid with

74

satinwood, or painted in different colours. The ruling idea,
of course, was to make the furniture harmonize with the
decorations of the rooms in which it was to be placed, and
that accounts for many expressions of the Adam style otherwise difficult to understand. Of original Adam furniture

FIG. 68. SIDEBOARD IN THE ADAM STYLE

very little is to be seen. In the South Kensington Museum
there are but three pieces, though there are architectural
productions by the brothers in the form of mantelpieces.
Sideboards, sometimes with serpentine fronts, sometimes
straight with square tapered legs, bookcases, cabinets,
screens, clock cases, chairs, etc., all were produced, as well

75

as bedsteads; in fact, everything necessary to the preservation of harmony between the architecture and decoration of a room and its contents.

The brothers Adam published a number of works on architecture, but it is beyond our scope to devote anything like detailed description to them. Of their decorative schemes, Robert Adam writes—

We have introduced a great diversity of ceilings, friezes and decorated pilasters, and have added grace and beauty to the whole by a mixture of grotesque stucco, and painted ornaments, together with the flowing rainceau, with its fanciful figures and winding foliage.

Among the various ornaments used by the brothers Adam were octagons, hexagons, ovals, rounds, lozenge-shaped panels, husks, fans, the sphinx, Greek and Roman vases, wreaths, honeysuckle, medallions with figures—the medallions sometimes draped—festoons, fauns, cupids, goats, eagle-headed grotesques, drapery, ribbons, caryatides, mythological subjects, ram's heads, lion's and eagle's claws for feet, griffins, sea-horses, pateras, etc., and draped figures.

In Robert Adam's day, furniture designing as apart from architecture was, to say the least, uncommon. Things have changed now, and changed so utterly and entirely that we can hardly realize the conditions which led the designers of the eighteenth century to write treatises on architecture as introductions to their volumes. Even amid a mass of such matter, however, there are gems to be found indicative of the spirit of the designer. Thus, Robert Adam writes—

If we have any claim to approbation, we found it on this alone—that we flatter ourselves we have been able to seize, with some degree of success, the beautiful spirit of antiquity, and to transfuse it with novelty and variety, through all our numerous works.

With the exception of those cases where French influence led to gilding chairs or such like, Robert Adam's claim may be freely admitted.

76

FIG. 69. WRITING CABINET IN THE ADAM STYLE

As architects they carried out much important work. For Londoners, the Adelphi Terrace remains a monument to their memory, and all who have visited the Savage Club will. remember the splendid specimens of their work visible within the building. A great number of their original drawings are to be seen in the Sir John Soane's Museum, and are well worthy of inspection by anyone who desires a closer acquaintance with Adam designs.

But little need be said of our illustrations. They will give our readers a comprehensive idea of the work of the brothers Adam and should enable them to identify the style.

The general impression one gets from Adam furniture is of its dignity and its grandeur. As to whether or not it is likely to exercise any considerable influence on modern styles it is exceedingly difficult to say. Unquestionably, its influence is felt in many modern productions, as, indeed, all great work of the present day partakes in a greater or less degree of the work of masters of a bygone period. Beyond that, however, it is pretty clear that furniture and decoration in the Adam style, pure and simple, are in very little demand now. Indeed, it is not perhaps too much to say that modern taste is in an opposite direction, cleaving to a simplicity of ornament or even a total absence of ornament, quite foreign to Adam ideas.

Mr. Percy Fitzgerald, in a lecture on Robert Adam, gave an eloquent testimony to the merits of the designer. A brief quotation from his appreciation will not be out of place here. He said that Robert Adam was one of the most wonderfully endowed men of his generation, a man who was filled with the fullest artistic instinct—one of whom it might well be said that everything he touched he adorned, and one who by instinct reached things which it took others years to effect. Adam was an artist. Discussing Adam's accomplishments, the lecturer pointed out that he was first an architect

FIG. 70. WARDROBE IN THE ADAM STYLE

who designed and built public buildings, noblemen's palaces and country houses, squares, streets, private houses, theatres. Next he was a decorator, one of the most beautiful and ornamental. He decorated his own houses. His decoration being structural, and in relief—not painted—it was inseparable from his buildings. That explains much, as we have already pointed out, and it must never be forgotten in estimating the value of the Adams' work in furniture designing.

Though there have not been lacking artistic critics who find Adam designs " flimsy and effeminate," we venture the opinion that such a verdict does not do justice to the talented brothers. One architect defending the pure Greek fashion, said that the Adam style was in reality a contrast to the classical, and was introduced by Robert Adam,

whose corrupt taste had invented a style which contained all the worst peculiarities of the worst class of ornamentation and composition ; it had its numerous admirers, and unfortunately was extensively practised. In some happy hour he is stated to have made one design of merit for Lord Scarsdale, viz., Kedlestone, which he carried into execution and which, as a whole, is considered to be a splendid composition.

The average reader will feel that such criticism is unjustifiable. So far from it being correct to say that Adam decoration " contained all the worst peculiarities of the worst class of ornamentation," modern authorities freely admit that the style, whether in popular demand for the moment or not, contains artistic merit of the highest order.

We remarked earlier in this chapter that the Adam style has been referred to as " an English edition of Louis Seize," and perhaps that gives us, in a phrase, a correct indication of the general tendency of the mode. Keen students of classical art, the brothers Adam modified the stately into the pretty and the dainty. One result is that Adam designs, whilst sometimes containing too great a measure of detail to give the best effect in large halls or *salons*, are eminently

suitable to smaller apartments or boudoirs. It will be remembered that precisely the same feature distinguishes the

FIG. 71. CHINA CABINET IN THE ADAM STYLE

Louis Seize style. Hence, for drawing-rooms, the Adam
decoration is perfect. There is a lightness and delicacy about
it particularly appropriate to the atmosphere of such; and
whatever measure of popularity there may be in store for

Adam furniture in the future, will, in all probability, lie in this direction.

The curious may be interested to note the attitude of Dr. Johnson toward the work of the brothers Adam, as recounted by Boswell. The good doctor's antipathy to Scotsmen is well known, and he expressed irritation because Robert Adam showed a preference for employing his own countrymen.

Why, now, the Adams are as liberal-minded men as any in the world; but I don't know how it is, all their workmen are Scotch!

Later in the biography, however, Boswell records that on viewing again some of Adam's work, Dr. Johnson

thought better of it to-day than when he saw it before; for he had lately attacked it violently.

Was not the real art in the work overcoming the great man's prejudice?

CHAPTER VIII

THE HEPPELWHITE STYLE

WE live in an age when the personal element occupies pre-eminently the place of importance. If we read a great book we would know the details of the life of the writer; if we see a great picture we must know something of the painter's

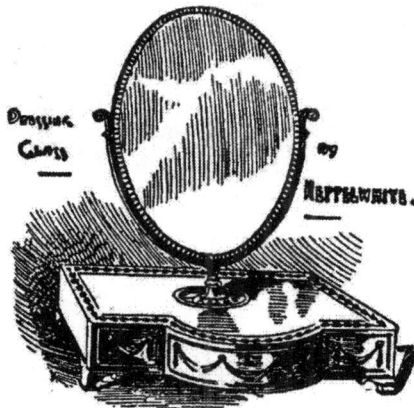

FIG. 72

life-story. And so it is with the men whose names have come down to us as standing for great recognized styles in furniture. It is not enough that we speak of the Heppel-white style—we would know who was Heppelwhite, what manner of man was he, and how did he live and move and have his being. Whilst freely admitting the legitimacy of the demand, we regret the inability to meet it in anything like an adequate degree. Times have changed. When, in the latter part of the eighteenth century " Messrs. A. Heppel-white & Co., cabinet-makers and upholsterers," lived, traded, and flourished, people cared more about what they

83

could produce than who they were, and their singular heed-
lessness of the inquisitiveness that was to be born a hundred
years later has robbed us of practically all the interesting
and instructive personalia which otherwise might have been
ours to-day.

Yet of not quite all the facts are we deprived. We have
already committed ourselves to the statement that there

FIG. 73

was a firm of " A. Heppelwhite & Co.," and we have pinned
our faith to the belief that they traded and flourished. That
is not much, but it is something. And to it we may add a
little that is not entirely groundless speculation. This
Heppelwhite was a man of like passions as ourselves. His
totally unjustifiable depreciation of Chippendale is evidence
enough of that. In that matter, however, Heppelwhite does
not stand alone, for who does not well remember the scornful
terms used by Sheraton in his references to the work of the
same great designer? Yet Thomas Chippendale has successfully stood the test of time—the most severe of all tests
—and, together with his critics, lives to-day as a master of
decorative and furnishing art.

84

Again, we know with tolerable certainty that " A. Heppelwhite & Co." flourished. Who but a flourishing firm could have produced the *Cabinetmaker and Upholsterer's Guide, or Repository of Designs for Every Article of Household Furniture in the Newest and Most Approved Taste*, published in 1788, by Messrs. I. & J. Taylor, Holborn, W.C., " opposite Great Turnstile "? This work is a monument of exquisite

FIG. 74

designs, including, as the authors claim, " a great variety of patterns." We shall have occasion to refer more fully to this volume later. We only refer to it now as some evidence of the flourishing condition of the authors.

Beyond these bare indications, we know practically nothing of Heppelwhite or the " Co.," save that we may with confidence deduce a skilled and talented craftsman, well in touch with the needs and the tastes of his day, and if at times content to pander to popular demands, to the degradation of his art and the obscuring of his own personality, yet displaying a genuine striving after the highest and the noblest that he saw. The result is a worthy one, and has come down to us in all that we know and understand as the " Heppelwhite style."

Turning to the work of Heppelwhite, it is not easy to summarize its distinguishing characteristics. Much of his work bears striking resemblance to that of Sheraton, particularly

SIDEBOARD   BY HEPPELWHITE.

FIG. 75

some articles executed in painted satinwood, inlaid. That Heppelwhite should have emphasized the peculiarly English character of his work is not to be wondered at. In this he joins hands with pretty nearly all the designers of eighteenth century furniture. Nor need we pass unduly harsh judgment on him when we find, upon closely examining his book, that much of his work is distinctly inspired or influenced by the Louis Seize style. Could not the same be truly urged against Chippendale and against Sheraton? Nor should we even say " urged against " but for the fact that in stilted

86

language, not free from suggestion of arrogance, these designers proclaim not only their English exclusiveness, but their undoubted superiority over all their competitors. Even so, two considerations induce us to temper our justice with

FIG. 76. HEPPELWHITE CHAIR

a very generous allowance of mercy. The first is found in the reflection that the men of our own day are not above re-dressing continental inspirations in garments singularly British. The second is found in the fact that the books published by these men of the eighteenth century were to some extent catalogues for advertising purposes, and not academic or learned treatises on furniture generally. They,

87

therefore, often included lines only justified by their good selling capacity.

Having said so much, however, we must put aside the claim of Heppelwhite that his designs are entirely English, and chronicle the fact that some of his best results were achieved by a skilful and artistic blending of the later

FIG. 77. HEPPELWHITE CHAIR

Louis XV and Louis XVI styles. His shield back chair, for instance, is indisputably French, as also is much of the detail of his decoration. The tapered legs of the Louis Seize style he used freely, whilst many of his beautiful panels in polished mahogany or satinwood are to be credited to Roentgen or Jean François Riesener rather than to any influence on this side of the channel.

May it not, moreover, be truly said that Heppelwhite, in common with all men, was indebted to those who had gone before, and with whose work he was more or less familiar? It is no reproach to him to point out, for instance, where his work has been coloured by that of the brothers Adam. It is a natural evolution, and with a true artist the latest expression will include the best of that of his predecessors. He will profit by their successes, take warning by their

FIG. 78. HEPPELWHITE CHAIR

failures. And so it was with Heppelwhite. He was simply no exception to the rule. It has been said that in the result Heppelwhite " was the link between the somewhat outrageous rococo of Chippendale and the severe lines of Sheraton," and perhaps that is as accurate an estimate of his precise work as it is possible to get in a few words.

Concerning the distinctive features of Heppelwhite's work, these may be briefly indicated. Chief among them, and of enduring popularity, stands the well-known easy chair with projecting " ears." The constant repetition of the Prince of Wales' feathers on his chair backs is another point, and this, as well as the carved wheat ears and graceful backs shaped like hearts, will be noticed in his designs. These are, perhaps, the most prominent of the distinctively Heppelwhite

FIG. 79. HEPPELWHITE CHAIR

features, though mention must be made of his practice of lacquering furniture as a foundation for decorative panels.

There is one striking difference between the work of Heppelwhite and that of Adam. In our chapter on the latter style we have commented upon the fact that the brothers Adam designed complete furnished rooms, and few of their productions are suitable for use in other surroundings. That is not true of Heppelwhite, whose furniture is harmonious in almost any environment.

It has been said that the inspiration of Heppelwhite is to

90

be found in the classic revival which was gaining ground at the time of the publication of the *Cabinetmaker and Upholsterer's Guide*, and that the movement to introduce the art of Italy into the manufactures of this country explained the peculiar features of his furniture. That is only partially

FIG. 80. HEPPELWHITE CHAIR

true, however; no man can escape altogether from the current influences of his day, and the Italian is easily traceable —indeed, is often particularly prominent—in Heppelwhite decoration. But beyond that, and beyond the French influence, is an originality attributable justly to no borrowed source of origin, but to be credited to the craftsman himself. That adaptation should be recognizable is no reproach. The merit is in the adaptation and in the combination of the best that the past has to yield with the truly artistic in the

91

inspiration of the designer's own period. It is thus that the "Heppelwhite style" is a style at all.

We have yet to discuss the book published by "A. Heppelwhite & Co.," to which reference has been made in the foregoing.

The *Cabinetmaker and Upholsterer's Guide* was published in 1788, and though copies of the original are scarce, a capital reproduction was issued a few years ago by Messrs. Batsford, of High Holborn. This book is a monument of design and fit to rank with any such volume published. It contains twenty-four pages of "Preface" and 124 sheets of designs, on which sheets are presented upwards of 300 separate designs. The beauty of these designs may be illustrated by saying that there are hardly any designs in the whole book which could not with profit be made up in the present day. Perhaps the most useless sheet in the volume is one of which the compilers were most proud—we mean the "Plan of a Room, showing the proper distribution of the furniture." This room is set out in a manner most unlikely to commend itself to-day. There is a geometrical correctness about it quite opposed to our modern notions of a drawing-room. We do not measure the length of the room and then place the chairs exactly equidistant from each other.

Apart from this, the book is rich in beautiful designs, and the articles depicted cover the widest variety and include chairs, stools, sofas, sideboards, pedestals and vases, knife boxes, desks and bookcases, secretaires, tables of every description, trays, dressing glasses and tables, chests of drawers, commodes, wardrobes, brackets, fire-screens, beds, lamps, cornices, etc. Each plate is referred to in some descriptive matter in the first part of the book. Of the designs in detail, we can say nothing. They are far too numerous for our space. The illustrations accompanying this chapter (and

which need little comment) will be sufficient for our purpose
now, which is to illustrate every phase of Heppelwhite design. In one or another of the designs we give will be found
pretty nearly every expression of the great designer's work.

The preface to Heppelwhite's book is interesting in the
same sense that we are interested by the stilted phrases used

FIG. 81. HEPPELWHITE CHAIR

by other eighteenth-century designers. They amuse us more
than they instruct. But we do not forget that it was expected of them to write in this strain. Some good illustrations of this method are to be found in the book under notice.
The opening sentence runs—

To unite elegance and utility, and blend the useful with the agreeable
has ever been considered a difficult but an honourable task. How far we
have succeeded in the following work it becomes us not to say, but rather

to leave it, with all due deference, to the determination of the public at large.

The Preface then proceeds to hope that the book will be found "useful to the mechanic and serviceable to the gentleman." The customary depreciation of the artists who had gone before is not lacking, and in grandiose language Heppelwhite goes on to say—

The mutability of all things, but more especially of fashions, has rendered the labours of our predecessors in this line of little use: nay, at this day, they can only tend to mislead those foreigners who seek a knowledge of English taste in the various articles of household furniture.

This criticism, of course, has been totally discredited by time. There is a suggestion of modesty in the concluding words—

Though we lay no claim to extraordinary merit in our designs, we flatter ourselves they will be found serviceable to young workmen in general and occasionally to more experienced ones.

This tone of humility is not always preserved. Describing Plate 79, it is said of a reflecting dressing table—

This is the most complete dressing table made, possessing every convenience which can be wanted, or mechanism and ingenuity supply.

We naturally turn to this prodigy and find that it hardly justifies the praise bestowed upon it. Indeed, many people would now term it a singularly awkward and inelegant structure. *Sic transit gloria mundi!*

We cannot refrain from quoting Heppelwhite's estimate of his work in the production of this volume—

To residents in London, though our drawings are all new, yet, as we designedly followed the latest or most prevailing fashion only, purposely omitting such articles whose recommendation was mere novelty, and perhaps a violation of all established rule, the production of whim at the instance of caprice, whose appetite must ever suffer disappointment if any similar thing had been previously thought of; we say, having regularly avoided those fancies, and steadily adhered to such articles only as are of general use and service, one principal hope for favour and encouragement

94

will be in having combined near 300 different patterns for furniture in so small a space, and at so small a price. In this instance we hope for reward.

So far as we know, that hope was not in vain.

Several of our illustrations are original Heppelwhite designs. In his book, Heppelwhite did not think it necessary

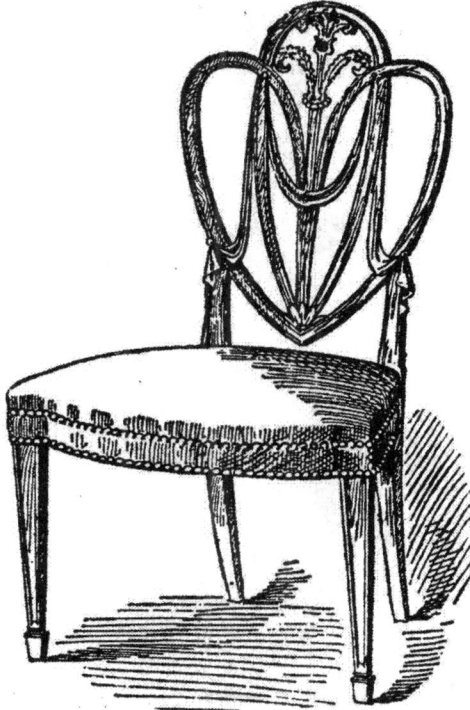

FIG. 82. HEPPELWHITE CHAIR

to give much description of his drawings to aid the craftsman in making them up. For instance, of the sideboard we reproduce on page 86, all that he says is that it is a design for a

sideboard without drawers, the ornaments to the front of which may be carved, painted or inlaid with various coloured woods.

95

Of the hanging book-shelves (on page 85), Heppelwhite says they are

designs for fretwork. These are often wanted as book-shelves in closets or ladies' rooms; they also are adapted to place china on; should be made of mahogany.

FIG. 83. HEPPELWHITE CHAIR

Of the window seat (on page 84), he says it is

of mahogany, carved, with furniture of an elegant pattern festooned in front. Will produce a very pleasing effect.

These examples will serve to show that Heppelwhite assumed much practical knowledge on the part of his readers.

Heppelwhite says in this volume—

The general dimension and proportion of chairs are as follows: Width in front 20 in., depth of the seat 17 in., height of the seat frame 17 in.; total height about 3 ft. 1 in.

96

He naïvely adds—

other dimensions are frequently adopted, according to the size of the room or pleasure of the purchaser.

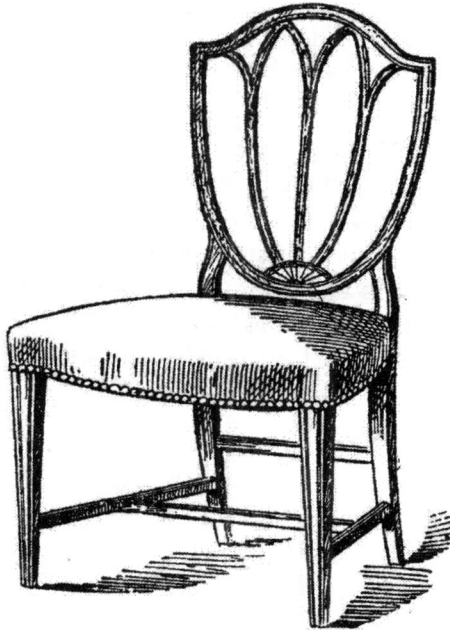

FIG. 84. HEPPELWHITE CHAIR

He recommends that his designs of chairs should be made up in mahogany

with seats of horse hair, plain, striped, chequered, etc., at pleasure, or cane bottoms with cushions.

It reads strangely to us to find Heppelwhite justifying the sideboard. The universal popularity won by this article causes us at times to forget that it was not always regarded as an essential in the furnishing of a dining-room.

The great utility of this piece of furniture (writes Heppelwhite) has procured it a very general reception, and the conveniences it affords render a dining-room incomplete without a sideboard.

We conclude our review by quoting Heppelwhite's estimate of two important rooms.

The proper furniture for a drawing-room and for a dining-room or parlour being thus pointed out, it remains only to observe that the general appearance of the latter should be plain and neat, while the former, being considered as a state room, should possess all the elegance embellishments can give.

There is a beauty in the Heppelwhite furniture that time does not destroy, because it contains the elements of permanence found in all true art. It is a style combining simplicity with great constructive skill, and though in point of mere popularity it is unlikely to prove a formidable rival to Chippendale or Sheraton designs, it will probably continue to find sufficient support to justify modern reproductions.

CHAPTER IX

THE LOUIS XVI STYLE

As in the case of Louis Quinze, it is not unprofitable, in dealing with Louis Seize, to note the association traceable between history and furniture designing. It may be said, in general terms, that the difference between the designs of

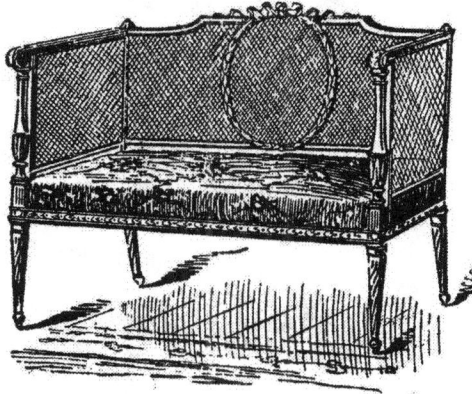

FIG. 85. MODERN LOUIS XVI SETTEE

the two reigns is a reflection of the difference in the character of the two monarchs. The suggestion, however, cannot be accepted as the explanation of the change, because it is not to be denied that the plainer lines distinctive of the Louis Seize style appear before 1774, the date when the ill-fated King came to the throne. Here, as on more than one previous occasion, we may remind the reader that the names given to the various styles must be regarded more as a matter of convenience than as an accurate description, inasmuch as it is never possible to draw a clear line of demarcation between one style and the style immediately preceding it.

The Louis Seize style is the result of the protest against the decadent forms of the rococo. Added to which the increasing embarrassment of the *noblesse* in matters financial,

FIG. 86. LOUIS XVI LYRE BACK CHAIR, DESIGNED FOR THE QUEEN'S BATHROOM AT THE PALACE OF FONTAINEBLEAU

compelling economy, or at any rate checking the prodigality of the earlier reign, demanded some movement in the direction of greater simplicity. The unhappy Louis XVI, himself an artificer of no mean ability, reigned (if his weak

FIG. 87. LOUIS XVI BAROMETER, IN MAHOGANY AND ORMOLU

amiability can be called reigning) only about eighteen years, the greater part of which time was a period of strife and trouble, for the country was in labour for the Revolution, and coming events were casting dark and ominous shadows before. The influence of Louis and his Queen, Marie Antoinette, upon furnishing style was all in the direction of comfort, elegance, and simplicity. The magnificent strength of Louis XIV, degenerating into the voluptuousness of Louis XV, was followed by this attempt to create a chaste

FIG. 88. MODERN LOUIS XVI SETTEE

and artistic style, and the result is the daintiness, even sometimes effeminacy, of the style Louis XVI.

Further, we now witness the growing popularity of the boudoir, and the consequent prominence of smaller pieces of furniture. A double influence tended to bring about this result. Louis XVI loved not the big Court gatherings and his Queen liked above all things a quiet country life, and the aristocracy had but little money to spend in expensive entertaining. "After us the deluge," said Louis Quinze, and the deluge was fast approaching. Great Court functions became rare, and even royal entertainments did not approach to the magnificence of the former reign. To the

102

social and political conditions of the time we owe the existence of some charming and delicate designs, such as are
found at the Château de Compiègne, at Fontainebleau, and

FIG. 89. LOUIS XVI FAUTEUIL, IN TAPESTRY

at Versailles. Straight lines now largely replaced curves and
the decorative details took form as rosettes, fruit, flowers,
fluting, shells, etc., where had been pagan deities and sensual
designs. Though perhaps the actual influence of Marie

103

Antoinette has been exaggerated, still it is worth remembering that it was her love of a simpler life which led to those sojourns at Trianon that were the cause of unjust scandal and ultimately, in a measure, of her death by the *guillotine*. Still, so far as it went, her influence was all on the side of delicate and artistic simplicity.

Another influence of the time was the discovery of Grecian

FIG. 90. SKETCHED FROM THE WALLACE COLLECTION

art treasures. Signs of the Greek are visible in much of the Louis Seize decoration.

Prominent among the designers of the period must be mentioned Riesener, Roentgen, and Gouthière. The work of the first-mentioned, particularly, is deserving of a high place in the records of art. His marqueteries, mounted exquisitely by Gouthière, are unequalled by anything similar in any age. In the Wallace Collection can be seen perhaps some of the finest specimens of the work of these men, such

104

as the splendid bureau said to have been made to the order of the King of Poland, Stanislas Leczinski, chiefly because of the letters " L. R." found on the sides, and which it is suggested stand for " Ludovicis Rex." This is open to dispute, however. It is strange to note that both Roentgen

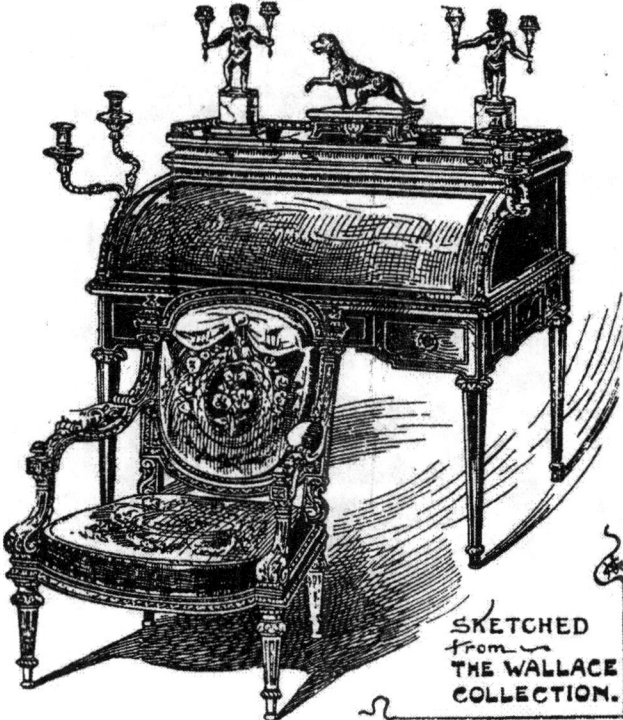

SKETCHED from THE WALLACE COLLECTION.

FIG. 91

and Riesener—the two best designers of the day—were Germans.

Excellent specimens of the furniture of this period are to be seen at South Kensington, including the work of some of the best makers of the time. Reference has already been made to the Wallace Collection, and to the places in France where the best expressions in Louis Seize furniture are to be

105

found. If some of these pieces are carefully examined, it will be seen that, although prices usually regarded as enormous were paid to the makers, it is probable that they could not be made to-day for a much lower figure. Only the costliest materials were used and the workmanship was masterly,

FIG. 92. LOUIS XVI CORNER CABINET, IN MAHOGANY, ORMOLU AND CHINESE LACQUER PANELS

some of the chased ormolu work being equal to the most delicate fashioning of jewellery.

The peculiar features, then, of the Louis Seize style are its simplicity as contrasted with Louis XV, the prevalence of straight lines and its daintiness. Its ornament is pastoral, though a *blasé* Court returning to nature could only effect a sort of artificial innocence. That is the peculiarity of this style. As one writer has said of the period, the aristocracy tried to cultivate the rusticity of the shepherds and shepherdesses, but made the attempt in tight corsage, Court

Fig. 93. Louis XVI Secretaire, in Mahogany, Ormolu and Lacquer Panels

dress, and high-heeled boots. The simplicity of the furniture and decoration strikes the same note of unreality or artificiality. It is beautiful—it is *charmant*—but it is not quite genuine. The players act well their rural parts, but they

107

are always actors. The flowing ribbons and " nature " ornaments dominating the style are daintier, more elegant, than
the originals.

During the period of the *Directoire* many of the treasures
of furnishing art were ruthlessly destroyed. In the madness
of the Terror it seemed patriotic to many to destroy anything connected with the hated aristocrats, and irreparable
acts of vandalism were committed in the name of liberty,
equality, and fraternity. It is true a small committee was
appointed to determine what of the furniture was worth
keeping as historically valuable and what should be abandoned, and thus some priceless goods were saved, but this
was but a spot of brightness in the black horizon. Even so,
the wholesale clearance was preparing the way for something new, and the work of destruction under the First
Republic made possible some rapid developments in furnishing when Napoleon inaugurated the style we shall
describe in another chapter.

Still, the process was costly and terrible. Lady Dilke
(whose work on French decoration and furniture in the
eighteenth century is invaluable and should be studied by
all interested in this period) says—

The work of destruction had been begun under the Revolution at the
promptings of the rage and shame which saw the symbols of social and
moral degradation in all that recalled the *ancien régime*. Unfortunately,
the forms in which it was intended to embody the aspirations after a
renewal of national life were reasoned out rather than felt. Considerations
wholly outside the province of art were encouraged to prevail in the
decision of matters regarding the construction of buildings, the decoration
and distribution of the interior.

To make room for the new " patriotic art," an auction
sale was held at the Palace of Versailles in August, 1793,
and the enormous collection of treasures there was scat-
tered. It is recorded that articles now almost priceless were
disposed of for insignificant sums, and two years later the

huge and costly building that had been the abode of wealth and luxuriousness was converted into a manufactory of arms.

It is further recorded that speculative purchasers at the Versailles auction, who acquired articles in the confident expectation of being able in the near future to dispose of

FIG. 94. MODERN LOUIS XVI LADY'S WORK TABLE

them at a very considerable profit, were disappointed, there being practically no market for the goods for some years. Thus, although becoming possessed of costly furniture at ridiculously low prices, the speculators incurred losses on their transactions. What changes are wrought in the passing of a few brief years! If we could but foresee them with prophetic eye and profit by our fore-knowledge!

Earlier in this chapter we have made passing allusion to the fact that Louis XVI was an artificer of no mean ability, and there is reason to believe that had he lived in happier

109

times Louis might have made his mark as a worker in metal. As it is, the picture of the weak and vacillating monarch, turning in the weariness of despair from affairs of State to find distraction in his hobby is a pathetic one indeed, and has been well drawn for us by Carlyle. One of the earliest views he gives us of the King (*French Revolution,* Vol. i) shows us His Majesty as a craftsman.

The simple young King, whom a Maurepas cannot think of troubling with business, has retired into the interior apartments; taciturn, irresolute; though with a sharpness of temper at times; he, at length, deter-

FIG. 95. LOUIS XVI COMMODE

mines on a little smith-work; and so, in apprenticeship with a Sieur Gamain (whom one day he shall have little cause to bless) is learning to make locks.

Later in the ill-fated monarch's career, after being compelled to come from Versailles to Paris, Carlyle writes of him, in October, 1789—

For his French Majesty, meanwhile, one of the worst things is that he can get no hunting. Alas, no hunting henceforth; only a fatal being-hunted! Scarcely, in the next June weeks, shall he taste again the joys of the game-destroyer; in next June, and never more. He sends for his

110

smith-tools; gives, in the course of the day, official or ceremonial business being ended, " a few strokes of the file," *quelques coups de lime*. Innocent brother mortal, why wert thou not an obscure substantial maker of locks; but doomed in that other far-seen craft, to be a maker only of world-follies, unrealities; things self-destructive, which no mortal hammering could rivet into coherence!

It was in November, 1792, when Gamain, alluded to above, disclosed the fact that Louis had hidden secret corre-

FIG. 96. LOUIS XVI COMMODE, IN THE LOUVRE MUSEUM, PARIS

spondence in an iron press (*armoire de fer*) " he and the royal apprentice fabricated." The discovery was destructive of the King's last chance of life. Henceforth his fate was sealed.

The influence of the amiable Marie Antoinette has been mentioned, and we have said it must not be overestimated. Still less should it be overlooked.

111

Says Carlyle—

Meanwhile the fair young Queen, in her halls of state, walks like a goddess of Beauty . . . Weber and Campan have pictured her, there within the royal tapestries, in bright boudoirs, baths, peignoirs, and the Grand and Little Toilette.

In those happy days at Versailles, and still happier at Trianon, the Queen displayed her delicate taste and artistic ability, and her influence was an important factor in the making of the style.

CHAPTER X

THE period between the execution of Louis Seize and the First Empire may be briefly passed over, as producing little of importance or significance in furniture designing. During the " Reign of Terror " it was hardly to be expected that the art of cabinet-making would flourish, and though there

FIG. 97. EMPIRE TABLE

is a decorative phase, denominated the *Directoire*, covering the few years in which were enacted the scenes of the Revolution, the division is an artificial one save as regards history alone, for the men of the Republic had neither time, inclination, nor talent for the development of the arts and crafts, though, indeed, they did appoint a commission of experts to decide what furniture was worth preserving from the general destruction of aristocratic possessions, as being historically valuable. The chief interest of the *Directoire* period for furnishers is to be found in the prosecution of certain *ébénistes* as being in the service of the reviled Louis Capet,

and the shifts they were driven to in order to clear themselves and prove their zeal for the Republic. We may come,
therefore, to the style called the Empire, contemporaneous

FIG. 98. EMPIRE COUCH

with Napoleon I, the well-recognized lines of which mark
the opening of the nineteenth century.

The Empire style was a return to the classic lines of Greek,
Roman, and Egyptian design. Chairs of Greek outline and

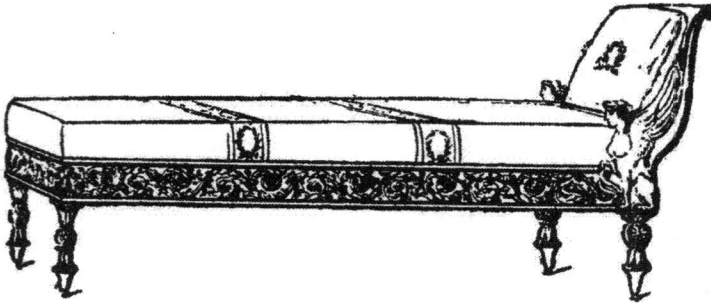

FIG. 99. EMPIRE COUCH

the detail of Roman decoration are prominent at this period.
Typical Empire ornament includes winged figures of various
forms emblematic of liberty, Greek vases, laurel wreaths,
lyres, the warrior's helmet, and the dove.

Mahogany was the wood chiefly employed in making the

114

furniture of this period, and with the heavy bronze and gilt mounting usually coupled with this style, the pieces present a most handsome appearance. Stateliness and dignity are features of the Empire style. Contrasted with the dainty Louis Seize designs, the transition is very marked. It is as though one stepped out of a beautiful and cosy boudoir in the castle of Marie Antoinette into the imperial dignity of a

FIG. 100. EMPIRE CHAIR AND TABLE, AT THE ESCURIAL PALACE, SPAIN

great Roman hall. Perhaps the great little Napoleon, himself a kind of nineteenth-century Caesar, favoured more the styles of antiquity than the effeminate furnishings that preceded his time of authority. The result is artistic, if at times a little stiff, and some of the Empire pieces are justly to be described as things of beauty and a joy for ever.

Between some of the styles it is at times difficult to draw a distinguishing line. It is never difficult to determine what

115

is Empire. The sudden return to the lines of Egypt, Rome, and Greece is plainly in evidence everywhere, as plainly, says one modern writer,

as if they all bore the plain Roman N, surmounted by a laurel wreath, or the Imperial Eagle which had so often led the French legions to victory.

FIG. 101. A GERMAN EMPIRE BEDSTEAD

We venture the opinion that there never was a style less in harmony with French temperament than the Empire style. Heaviness, solidity, and stately dignity are not characteristics of the Frenchman, and the lines of Napoleonic furniture, though gracefully artistic, seem to be, to a large extent, the expression of an artificial constraint. This view is strengthened by the fact that after the fall of Napoleon the Empire style fell quickly into disrepute, and even as all reactions lead more or less to excesses, so we have in the

116

French furniture of the middle of the nineteenth century the " baroque " or " debased rococo," in which all the worst features of Louis Quinze ornament and design were revived, without the talent of the great designers whose genius was the redeeming feature of the eighteenth-century productions.

In England the influence of the Empire furniture is apparent in many of Sheraton's designs, some of which, except for the absence of the metal decorations, might be genuine Empire pieces. But whereas in France inlaying and carving

FIG. 102. EMPIRE CHAIR   FIG. 103. EMPIRE GRAND PIANO

were practically discarded in favour of ormolu (lit. gilt or gold-moulded) ornamentation, in England inlay and carving were practised *par excellence* by Sheraton and his school.

The two names most prominent in this period are those of Jacob Desmalter, *ébéniste*, and Percier, the architect. These were employed by Napoleon in the work of refurnishing Malmaison, and on other important enterprises at the different palaces, including Versailles and the Tuileries. The most important work on decoration published during the Empire period was that of Beauvallet and Normand. This contains many admirable designs in the style. Another work

117

was that of Fontaine and Percier, in the preface of which the authors repudiate the French origin of the style, pointing out that their only merit is that of the adapter. Fontaine also published a history of the Palais Royal.

The foregoing, together with the illustrations of typical Empire designs given, will be sufficient to denote the peculiar features of this period. Strictly it is not a French style. It

FIG. 104. ARMCHAIR IN THE EMPIRE STYLE

is an attempt toward a French translation of classic art and, as such, was distinctly successful, the result being the creation of much that was of enduring beauty. The fact that numerous Empire pieces do not touch this high ideal is no reason for discrediting the style as a whole. The feature of the period is the beautifully shaped ormolu mounting, quite inconsistent with economy and certain to be degraded in the process of cheap reproduction. It is true that all styles are open to the same reproach and it is not reasonable to

118

appraise any era by its worst expressions. The classic simplicity of Greek and Roman art tends to give prominence to unworthy imitations when comparison is made. It is easier to counterfeit the ornate than the gems of stately art. That is why " sham " Empire reproductions are so often in bad taste and of unworthy workmanship.

FIG. 105. EMPIRE CABINET

FIG. 106. EMPIRE BOOKCASE

The influence of David, the artist, during the *Directoire* and Empire periods must not be overlooked. His genius was a potent factor in many ways in the work of adaptation, or perhaps we may say of creating the Empire style, for some of his efforts are more than modified copies of the classical. Under Napoleon he found sufficient recognition, and his official position gave him the opportunity to stamp his individuality upon the productions of his day.

119

It is unlikely that anything like a modern revival of the Empire style will take place. Despite the justly enduring

FIG. 107. EMPIRE CHAIR   FIG. 108. EMPIRE CHAIR

popularity of certain types and pieces, the resuscitation of the style as a whole is improbable. Modern tastes go not that way.

CHAPTER XI

L'ART NOUVEAU

WE have deemed it convenient to deal in this chapter with continental productions classified as Art Nouveau, reserving our next chapter for a consideration of British expressions of the style. This has become necessary because designers

FIG. 109. L'ART NOUVEAU CHAIRS

in this country struck out a line quite distinct from the continental, having characteristics of its own. Hence we give to native designs in this style the name of New Art as a denomination appropriately distinguishing them from their French, German, and Italian cousins.

A good deal of somewhat flippant criticism has been urged against l'Art Nouveau by some people in high places who should have known better. Thus one eminent artist has characterized the style as an

ebullition of crazy incompetency . . . the outcome of degeneracy . . . the mud mountain of rubbish daily and yearly heaped up by the

121

incompetent, social, amateur ass, who mistakes the praise of his fellow incompetents for his supply of new sensations to his equally diseased patrons. L'Art Nouveau, forsooth! Absolute nonsense! It belongs to the young lady's seminary and the "duffer's" paradise. (Mr. Alfred Gilbert, R.A., in the *Magazine of Art*.)

FIG. 110. L'ART NOUVEAU CHAIR

In the same journal, Mr. George Frampton, R.A., says—

I do not exactly know what it means. I believe it is made on the continent and used by parents and others to frighten naughty children.

Apart from the unnecessarily violent language of Mr. Gilbert, language that naturally robs his opinion of what critical value it might otherwise have possessed, and the feeble humour of Mr. Frampton, there are many people whose impatience with l'Art Nouveau, if less emphatically expressed, is none the less real. The fact is that the style

122

was one peculiarly liable to abuse, and the critics have too
often formed general conclusions from an observation of

FIG. 111. AN ITALIAN L'ART NOUVEAU SCREEN

particularly bizarre pieces. The real Art Nouveau had too
much of true beauty to be dismissed by reason of some
unbeautiful productions labelled with that name.

What was l'Art Nouveau? We will attempt an answer to
that question as briefly as possible.

123

In every progressive age there is more or less artistic restlessness, and the modern spirit of aestheticism found expression in France, and subsequently in other countries on the
continent, in this new and sometimes weird style. Its peculiar features may be indicated in a few sentences. Very

FIG. 112. L'ART NOUVEAU CHAIR, AT SOUTH KENSINGTON
MUSEUM

noticeable is the absence of straight lines except where they
are absolutely necessary. In many typical Art Nouveau
pieces, indeed, it would be difficult to find straight lines anywhere. Curves, bold and sweeping, sometimes tortuous, are
essential. Orthodox canons of construction are cast to the
winds; regular rules are abandoned, and *apparently* a course
is adopted in the production of designs the exact opposite
of that which necessitated geometrical calculation and an
124

unswerving devotion to scale. We say *apparently* this is so
because a closer examination of Art Nouveau furniture
quickly reveals the fact that the easy nonchalance is in

FIG. 113. L'ART NOUVEAU SIDEBOARD

reality effected by careful studiousness, and carelessness is
but on the surface.

The decoration employed is, like the outlines permitted,

125

bold and unconventional. Inlaying is frequently adopted, and executed with the greatest skill, often recalling the work of some of the past-masters in the art of marquetery. Occasionally florid and gross departures are evidenced, reminding

FIG. 114. ORIGINAL L'ART NOUVEAU CHAIR

us forcibly—too forcibly—of the rococo of Louis Quinze. But these must be regarded as an "abuse of liberty," and above and beyond all mere eccentricities, or unworthy reversions to decadent types, l'Art Nouveau presents features of attraction and originality certain, if anything is certain in furniture designing, to win for its best forms a permanence only achieved by real art.

Since the Empire style, French craftsmen have, in common perhaps with their brothers of other nationalities, produced

FIG. 115. L'ART NOUVEAU CABINET, AT SOUTH KENSINGTON MUSEUM

nothing of note (except along old lines) until the birth of l'Art Nouveau. The date of this interesting event cannot with definiteness be fixed, but the work of what has been called the Secessionist school may confidently be limited to the last forty years at the outside. It will be seen, therefore, that its progress has been extraordinary, and it is no

FIG. 116. L'ART NOUVEAU BEDSTEAD, AT SOUTH KENSINGTON MUSEUM

exaggeration to say that it is the dominant note in decorative schemes on the continent to-day. At one time even art metal work in this style, of great beauty of outline, met the eye everywhere, and in Paris the principal shop fronts were largely fashioned in the popular mode. Apart from reproductions of classic styles, for which an increasing and regular demand is always to be counted upon, practically nothing else was then made, except, of course, in the cheaper grades.

128

But l'Art Nouveau did not retain its early forms. There was soon a noticeable absence of the extreme patterns, many of which were not inappropriately described as " rampant hooliganism of art." Such disappeared, or at any rate were no longer to be found in the work of craftsmen of repute.

FIG. 117. L'ART NOUVEAU BEDSTEAD

The productions took on a chastened form, truly artistic, but properly describable by no other term than l'Art Nouveau.

Our view is that this style went through a gradual evolution—a process of natural selection had been at work, and we then witnessed the result in the survival of the fittest. We further venture the opinion that l'Art Nouveau is not so much a style in itself as a method of treatment, a mode of expression, and any style can be treated in the Art Nouveau manner. The "hooliganism" in l'Art Nouveau is easily explained. When the idea was new, and whilst yet the artist was feeling his way with care, the mediocre, with the impulsiveness of true mediocrity, rushed ahead

FIG. 118. L'ART NOUVEAU BUFFET

and brought forth wild and impossible productions which called out upon them, and justly, the ridicule and impatient condemnation of the casual observer. But meantime the artist was still at work, and it is this undercurrent that is really representative of the true spirit of l'Art Nouveau, and assisted the new movement in establishing itself upon the sure foundation of the beautiful. We, therefore, protest

130

FIG. 119. "CHINESE" L'ART
NOUVEAU CABINET

FIG. 120. L'ART NOUVEAU
SHOP PIER GLASS

FIG. 121. INLAID L'ART NOUVEAU
TABLE

FIG. 122. L'ART NOUVEAU
CHAIR

against the hasty criticism that reckons only with a part of the facts of the case, ignoring the best and seeing only the unworthy. Many of the critics will yet come to see the error of their ways, and live to bow before the spirit of l'Art Nouveau as a modern chastening influence, the *Zeitgeist* come to carry the art of former days to a higher level.

FIG. 123. L'ART NOUVEAU CHAIR

We have said that any style may be expressed in l'Art Nouveau methods. We have seen it in Paris applied to refined Louis XV in the regime of Madame de Pompadour. We have seen many Louis designs, which are really Louis, treated in l'Art Nouveau manner. Perhaps this inspiration —for inspiration it assuredly is—is one presenting great possibilities in this country. Perhaps we have here a suggestion that may lead to the final answer of the oft-asked question, "Has it come to stay?"

132

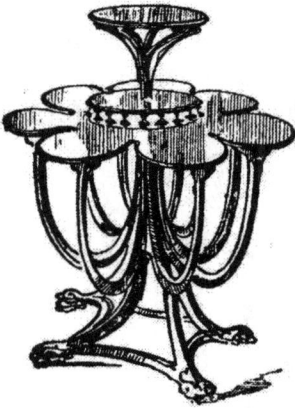

FIG. 124. L'ART NOUVEAU FIVE
O'CLOCK TEA TABLE

FIG. 125. L'ART NOUVEAU
TOILET TABLE

FIG. 126. " CHINESE " L'ART
NOUVEAU CABINET

FIG. 127. NOUVEAU BRIC-A-
BRAC PEDESTAL

The origin of the Art Nouveau movement is not beyond dispute. Some say it really originated in this country, that the suggestion was caught up on the continent, developed (distorted, say the critics), and sent back in such forms that

FIG. 128. ORIGINAL L'ART NOUVEAU CHAIR

it was beyond recognition. It may be so, but it is much more likely that similar strivings after the new in art were going on independently in many countries. The British results we discuss in our next chapter. L'Art Nouveau, as we understand it, owes but little to the influence of British designers. It is essentially a product of foreign genius, and
134

FIG. 129. L'ART NOUVEAU SHOW
TABLE

FIG. 130. L'ART NOUVEAU
DRESSING TABLE

FIG. 131. L'ART NOUVEAU
FLOWER STAND

finds its home in France, Germany, Austria, and Italy. Sufficient evidence in support of this contention may be found in an examination of some of our illustrations, depicting articles that could only have been designed by foreigners. Their boldness and unconventionality are not British in any

FIG. 132. L'ART NOUVEAU CHAIR

sense, and these features rapidly disappear in British reproductions in the mode.

Of all the unjust criticism, perhaps the least accurate is the one that attributes " slavish imitation " to the Art Nouveau designers, for it is above all things a free style. Indeed, it is this very freedom that has led to the production of the horrible, for there are always those with whom

136

liberty will degenerate into licence. But the absolute freedom from all restraint that is permissible to the designer of Art Nouveau furniture offers the greatest temptation to the

FIG. 133. TWO L'ART NOUVEAU CHAIRS

artist to express *himself* with originality. Imitation is much more natural where a particular style is to be correctly depicted. With l'Art Nouveau there is no *correctness*—beauty

FIG. 134. L'ART NOUVEAU TABLES

is its one canon, and if the creation is beautiful, no one has a right to demand more of it.

L'Art Nouveau, though possessing beauty, could hardly become popular (in the ordinary acceptation of that term),

137

because the nature of its designs is such as to prohibit cheap reproduction. The high prices asked for some of the beautiful pieces in this style were not altogether due to novelty, or even to the employment of expensive designers, but to the actual cost of the material used and the workmanship necessitated. Where, at every point, the manufacturer meets with difficult curves and eccentric lines; where duplication is impossible and the skilled workman is needed for every

FIG. 135. L'ART NOUVEAU OCCASIONAL TABLE

detail; where the machine is useless and the apprentice worse than useless; where expensive inlaying is employed in almost prodigal profusion; where, in short, constructive difficulties abound and the most costly material has to be extravagantly cut up, cheapness is out of the question. It was thus certain that the more elaborate expressions of the Art Nouveau style must always remain the possessions of the comparatively wealthy. In its simpler forms, however, its graceful outlines have without doubt had influence. The end is not yet. The progressive movement is still going on,

138

and out of all the strife will come something better than we
have yet seen in this direction, as, we believe, anyone who

FIG. 136. L'ART NOUVEAU GILT SETTEE

carefully studies the Art Nouveau of the last five years will
readily admit.

FIG. 137. L'ART NOUVEAU
NEWSPAPER STAND

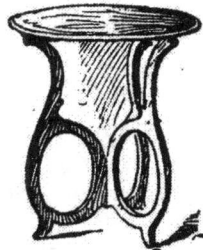

FIG. 138. L'ART NOUVEAU
TABLE

We are able to present a large number of illustrations of
articles of furniture in this style, some good and some the
reverse. We have thought well to reproduce some designs

139

for the sole purpose of showing " how not to do it." In this
category we may fairly include some of the chairs exhibited
at the Düsseldorf Exhibition (1902), and according to the
individual taste the line will be drawn, excluding some of
the other pieces illustrated from the " possible " in l'Art
Nouveau. We do not forget that it has been urged against

FIG. 139. L'ART NOUVEAU TABLE

Germany that some of the worst designs were perpetrated
there. One recent writer on l'Art Nouveau says—

To the German, of course, it was a godsend. The modern German
artist has not been conspicuous for originality, but here he found his
chance of freeing himself from the reproach of dullness; he had but to
throw the reins on the neck of his Rosinante, and find himself in the first
flight of l'Art Nouveau. There is no such outrageous person as the respect-
able bourgeois on the loose; and the German having once broken away,
appears to be fairly wallowing in orgies of artistic intemperance.

Again are we disposed to protest that general conclusions
must not be so readily drawn from particular instances. The
" wallowing in orgies of intemperance " has not always been

confined to the Art Nouveau designer. The expression might with greater justice be applied to some of his critics. At the same time it must be admitted that such designs as, for instance, the chairs reproduced below, are calculated to call forth ridicule. But little can be said in defence of such grotesque specimens. They present no graceful lines,

FIG. 140. L'ART NOUVEAU CHAIRS SHOWN AT THE DÜSSELDORF EXHIBITION

and the obtrusive suggestion of " bandiness " is not pleasing. We had the opportunity of closely examining the originals at the Düsseldorf Exhibition (1902), but there is only one good quality we can ascribe to them, and that is that we found them very strong.

That there is likely to be any further development in this somewhat objectionable direction we do not believe. Indeed, it is pretty apparent that the speculative wildness and irresponsible daring manifested in such designs as these

141

Düsseldorf chairs have even already met with a reception so chilling as to discourage designers from experimenting any further on similar lines. The most outrageous forms of art, or the most flagrant offences against all art's recognized canons, may with a tolerable degree of certainty count upon a measure of support from the uncritical and those devoid of the artistic sense, of whom there are sufficient numbers to tempt

FIG. 141. L'ART NOUVEAU CHAIR

the impecunious genius to exploit " fresh fields and pastures new." Is this not true in all branches of art? Is the painter exempt from the seductive influence of the wealthy patron without taste, who will purchase anything "extreme," in the belief that by so doing he is acquiring a treasure the like of which is possessed by no one else? But the triumph of ignorance is temporary, and l'Art Nouveau has advanced beyond that stage. The forms in this style that are to endure go not that way.

In this particular, furniture is to be subjected to a severer test than, say, pictures. An extraordinary, a horrible, or a

grotesque painting may well, and often does, give satisfaction, where an extraordinary, horrible, or grotesque piece of

FIG. 142. L'ART NOUVEAU
CHAIR

FIG. 143. L'ART NOUVEAU WORK
TABLE

furniture would be promptly discarded. If our furniture
was made for the purpose of being looked at periodically

FIG. 144. L'ART NOUVEAU UMBRELLA STAND

for a brief moment, the conditions would be altered. As it
is, we demand that furniture shall satisfy us at all times, in

143

FIG. 145. AN ITALIAN L'ART NOUVEAU CABINET

season and out of season, and the " hooligan " design that attracted our attention at an exhibition and called a smile to our lips—nay, even that excited our admiration, would not be suited to the daily inspection and familiar use to

FIG. 146. A KEY HOLDER AND BRUSH HOLDER IN L'ART NOUVEAU STYLE

which we subject our chosen furniture. And as the inexorable law of supply and demand reaches even into the world of art, the supply of bizarre designs may not unnaturally be expected to diminish to the disappearing point. Only that furniture will endure that has the power not only to please

145

FIG. 147. AN ITALIAN L'ART NOUVEAU CABINET

our artistic sense at the moment, but that possesses the necessary qualities to enable it to be to us as our daily bread. It must not become obnoxious by reason of constant use.

We have included in this chapter some designs in Art Nouveau metal work, partly because the style is one lending itself with particular appropriateness to treatment in metal, and partly because the illustrations given bear very closely upon furniture itself. The metal embellishments of Art Nouveau furniture are a feature of the mode, and, as indicating the lines upon which continental artists were working, our drawings will be very interesting.

Apart from wild exaggerations and the merely eccentric, however, no one with artistic eye could examine all our illustrations and fail to find the note of real beauty strongly represented. There is a graceful freedom writ large on the style that is more than charming. If its more extreme designs cause us uneasiness, its restrained and chastened expressions give us real pleasure. The style did, through much tribulation, overcome many of its youthful follies, and sowed its wild oats. It was not endangered by mere ridicule or abuse, and one did not need much prophetic boldness to foretell for it some artistic future. The best men on the continent worked upon it. Their work probably helped to develop a style the beauty of which shall entitle it to rank with the daintiest of furniture of any previous period.

CHAPTER XII

BRITISH NEW ART

WE have, in the preceding chapter, dealt with l'Art Nouveau style as exhibited on the continent, thereby shortening our task with regard to British New Art. Apart from the question—of academic interest only—whether the style originated here, went to the continent and returned, or originated

FIG. 148. A NEW ART DRESSING TABLE

abroad and was imported into this country, we may safely say that it was only since its " return " that it made any real mark in Great Britain. If no other reason for the statement existed, the mere fact that the earliest New Art designs were the most fantastic would in itself be strong presumptive evidence of its correctness. Continental New Art, particularly

148

in its earlier stages, presented outlines never designed, or contemplated, by British designers; and its forms, coming over here, were transformed to meet British tastes. Offensive exaggerations and weirdness of outlines were removed, and in place of these the style was developed in a chaste and restrained manner, more suitable to our temperament.

FIG. 149. NEW ART CHINA CABINET

William Morris has defined the British position on this subject inimitably. He wrote—

For us to set to work to imitate the minor vices of the Borgias, or the degraded and nightmare whims of the *blasé* and bankrupt French aristocracy of Louis XV's time, seems to me merely ridiculous. So I say our furniture should be good citizens' furniture, solid and well made in workmanship, and in design should have nothing about it that is not easily defensible, no monstrosities or extravagances, not even of beauty, lest we weary of it. As to matters of construction, it should not have to depend on the special skill of a very picked workman, or the super-excellence of his glue, but be made on the proper principles of the art of joinery: also I think that, except for very movable things like chairs, it should not be

149

so very light as to be nearly imponderable; it should be made of timber rather than walking-sticks.

That is an admirable word-picture of the British New Art movement, and indications are plentiful that it is along that line that the way of permanence lies.

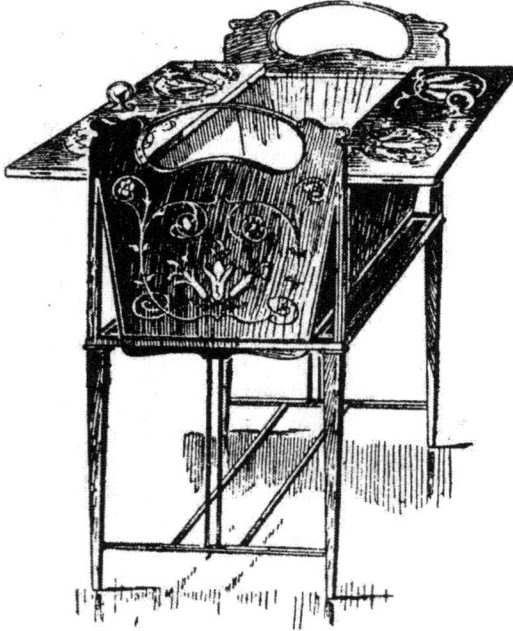

FIG. 150. NEW ART WORK TABLE

The style goes by many names. Sometimes it is denominated New Art, more often it is called Quaint or Modern, whilst some describe it as Arts and Crafts. In America it is known as Mission. But by whatever name it is called, the features of the style itself are readily recognizable. Artistic simplicity and the absence of ornate decoration or carving are its chief marks. Much furniture in New Art style has been made in fumigated oak, but other woods are equally appropriate to its best forms. The decoration consists of

150

inlaying chiefly, or the use of repoussé art metal work, or fancy tiles in art colourings. In this way some beautiful results have been obtained.

In the newer designs it is plain that the dictates of William Morris have been followed. "Good citizens' furniture" is

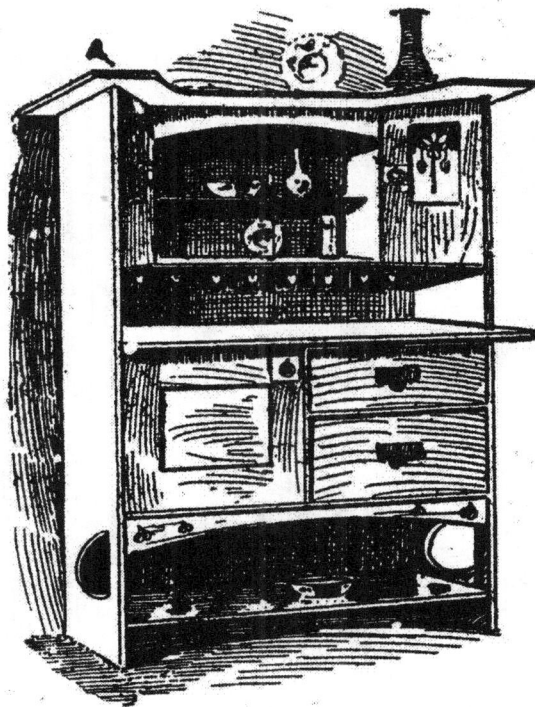

FIG. 151. NEW ART CHIFFONIER

suggestive of something with plenty of wood in it, and it is perhaps more likely that over-solidity, approaching to heaviness, is the danger of the British designer, rather than the lightness that is "nearly imponderable."

One great difference between the British and the continental New Art is that where the latter presents few straight lines, the former revels in unbroken rectangular outlines.

151

FIG. 152. NEW ART OR QUAINT BOOKCASE

The severity of many New Art pieces is very surprising considering the continental descent (if, indeed, that descent be admitted by our designers), and the only possible explanation is that the British designers and manufacturers evolved from l'Art Nouveau a distinct and original style coming down to

FIG. 153. NEW ART WARDROBE

us through Art Nouveau channels, but presently departing from the orthodox love of unorthodoxy that is the hall-mark of that style, and setting up artistic canons irreconcilable with the freedom of the system of curves, swirls, and blobs.

In America the movement followed closely on British lines. The Mission style was much nearer our New Art patterns than the continental Art Nouveau. If anything, it was ruder and simpler than the British furniture, and the

153

FIG. 154. NEW ART OR QUAINT BOOKCASE

advantages urged for it are cleanliness, durability, and that " it is not hard to understand." One American writer hoped that there would come

an opportunity to evolve from the Mission style a more elaborate style that shall be quite as much in keeping with American ideals and at the same time suitable for parlour use.

FIG. 155. DESIGN FOR A NEW ART CABINET

In this country that difficulty has long been solved. Avoiding the eccentricity, and in consequence missing much of the

155

real beauty, of the Art Nouveau, British designs include artistic pieces worthy to grace the most elegant drawing-room or boudoir.

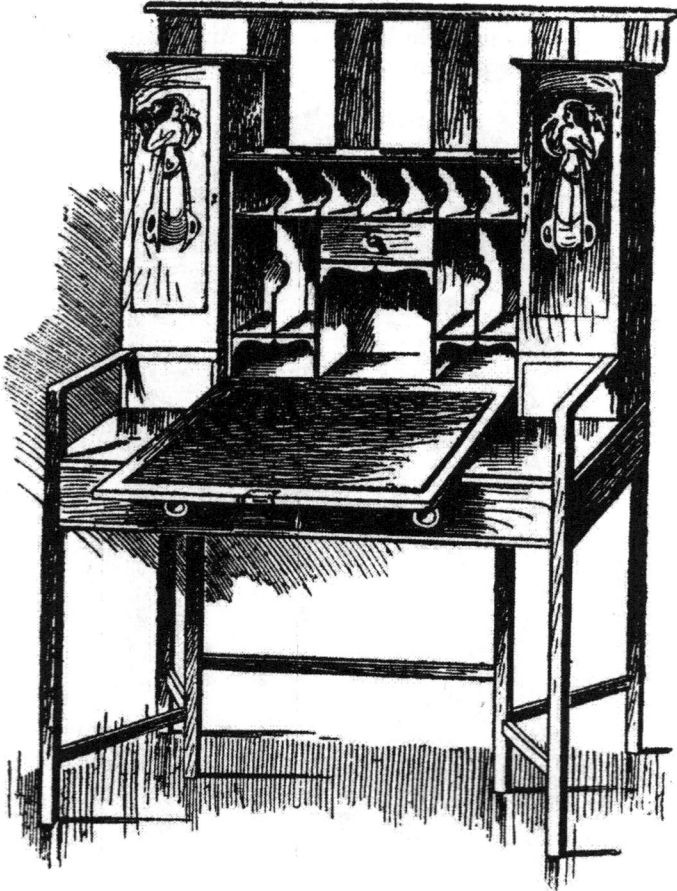

FIG. 156. NEW ART OR QUAINT WRITING TABLE

Another important difference between the British and the continental forms is the cost. As already pointed out, the Art Nouveau designs were, generally speaking, very expensive and, in their essential features, incapable of economical reproduction. The simpler, straighter lines of the British style not only satisfy our more sober taste, but render possible the manufacture of some of the finest designs at a very low cost. Herein the New Art style possessed an advantage, not only over its continental brother, but over the classic

FIG. 157. DESIGN FOR NEW ART CHAIR

styles also, because articles of equal quality as to material and workmanship could be sold at much lower prices in New Art designs than is the case with, say, Sheraton or Chippendale pieces. We say this fully recognizing the fact that certain designers found it possible to put very high prices on their productions, but in such cases the figure must be

157

regarded as an artificial one, because even with the more
elaborate typical New Art furniture the average manufacturer could reproduce facsimiles of high-priced pieces, in no
way inferior to the originals, at exceedingly moderate prices.
Such would not be possible with the average Art Nouveau

FIG. 158. DESIGN FOR NEW ART CHAIR

design. For this reason the New Art became popular in this
country in a sense in which it never could in France or
Austria. The (sometimes obtrusive) plainness of its lines;
the general appearance of genuine solidity, beloved by the
average Briton; and the absence of cheap and tawdry
decoration and villainously executed "carving," all go to
commend the style to the educated man. When to these
158

recommendations is added that of moderate cost, it is not surprising that the New Art should have quickly won for itself numerous supporters.

FIG. 159. NEW ART TABLE

It was not easy to predict with confidence what would be the future of the New Art in this country, but there were indications worth noting, suggesting the direction the movement would take. It is clear that the merely bizarre will find

159

FIG. 160. NEW ART TABLE

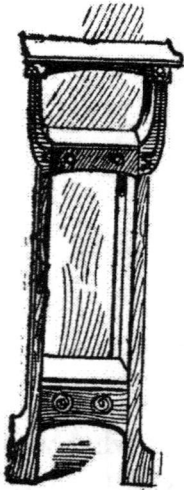

FIG. 161. NEW ART
PEDESTAL

FIG. 162. NEW ART
STATUARY TABLE

FIG. 103. NEW ART
TABLE

but small favour. The restrained forms are becoming more
popular every day. Eccentricity may create interest, but it

FIG. 164. DESIGN FOR A NEW ART CABINET

does not, in England, result in sales; and, after all, the production of furniture is a commercial matter. Very soon New

Art lines were on the market to which the critic could take no artistic exception. They were plain, perhaps, but they were dignified, and fulfilled the test of William Morris, by presenting no features that cannot readily be justified. Some notable examples, indeed, proved that excesses of plainness may be committed as well as excesses of " curves and swirls,"

FIG. 165. NEW ART LAMP STAND   FIG. 166. NEW ART STAND

and the result is quite as objectionable. There is nothing commendable in designing a piano after the fashion of a packing-case, or in seeking to introduce a rough and common milkmaid's stool into our drawing-rooms. Excess in this direction has called forth much ridicule, but must not blind us to the real New Art movement going on behind all mere extravagance and eccentricity of genius.

We suggested in the preceding chapter that l'Art Nouveau

162

might be regarded as a method of treatment possible to any
style. A glance at our illustrations will show that our designers promptly realized the truth of that proposition. Some
New Art pieces are distinctly Sheraton treated in New Art
fashion, and the result is far from being displeasing. Some
other classic styles may also be traced in recent New Art
designs.

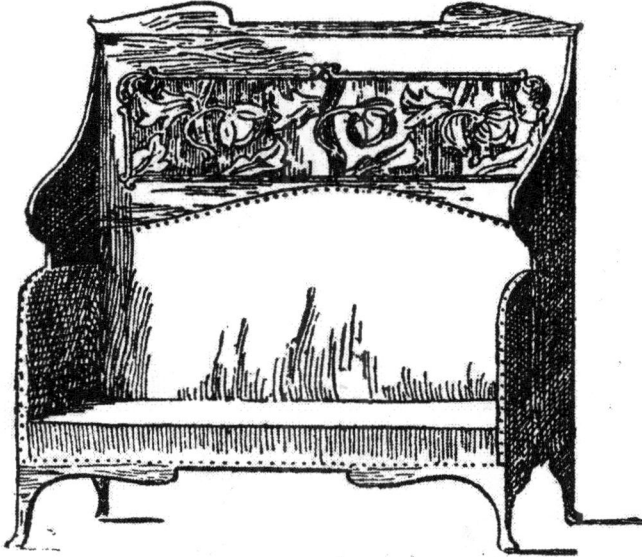

FIG. 167. NEW ART SETTEE

The style was likely to find permanent favour in this
country, though, of course, its lines were bound to undergo
some alterations. Combining, as it did, the qualities of simplicity, usefulness, and solidity, and permitting of comparatively inexpensive production, New Art furniture had an
undoubted influence on British furniture styles.

If the illustrations accompanying this chapter are carefully examined, perhaps the first impression conveyed will
be that some of the designs might without incongruity have

been classified as Art Nouveau. On the other hand, many continental designs are sufficiently British to justify their classification as New Art. In this country a good deal of work has been turned out on lines more or less foreign, but it is in the earlier New Art pieces that this is most noticeable. Latterly, British designers to a large extent

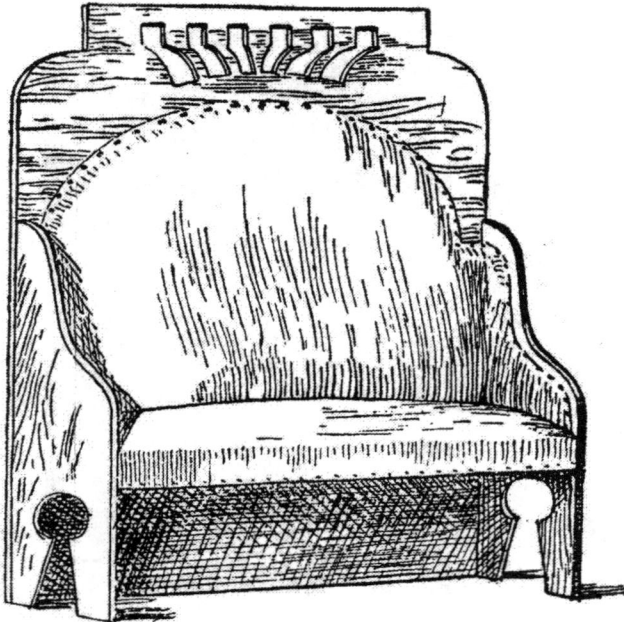

FIG. 168. NEW ART SETTEE

freed themselves from anything like foreign influence, dividing their attention between severe simplicity and a modification of eighteenth-century styles in accordance with New Art methods. Of the latter phase it would be possible to write at great length, for the subject is a fascinating as well as an important one. Sheraton designs, in particular, appear to lend themselves successfully to New Art treatment, and some exceedingly beautiful pieces of furniture have

164

been produced by the combination of New Art and Sheraton ideas. Early indications, however, appeared to point to the future popularity of the simpler New Art forms. For bedroom furniture these plain designs very quickly achieved a vogue little short of extraordinary when we consider how comparatively new they were, and in the dining-room they were fast winning an increasing popularity. It is useless to

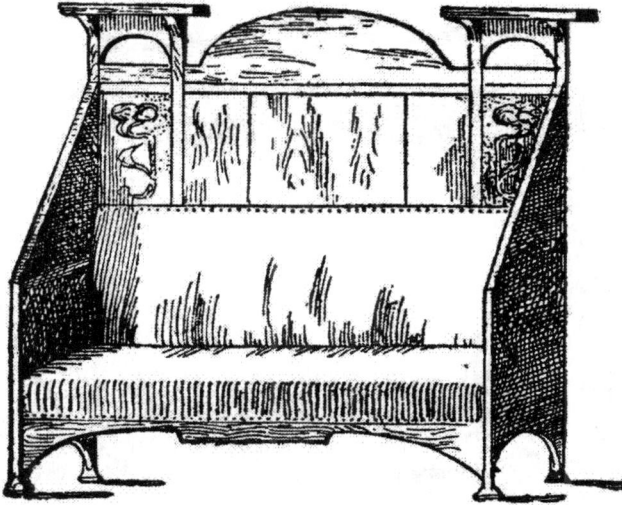

FIG. 169. NEW ART SETTEE

utter impatient criticisms or to attempt by extravagant abuse and unsympathetic denunciation to stay the tide. Equally useless is it to talk in pedantic strain of the decadent artistic faculty. The voice of the people, at any rate in matters furnishing, is more likely to be the voice of the artistic deity than is the academic utterance of the professional artist. At any rate, a style that has the capacity of satisfying popular needs, aesthetic as well as utilitarian, must possess merits of no mean order, and in the best New Art productions is it not possible to recognize some reflections of our national characteristics? Simplicity, strength, solidity—these are qualities appealing eloquently to the average Briton, and should he be called upon to choose between a sham elaboration of a French classic style, disguised under a British name, and a genuine piece of plain furniture, the simplicity of which is a guarantee of honesty, we have no hesitation in concluding that he will choose the latter. To

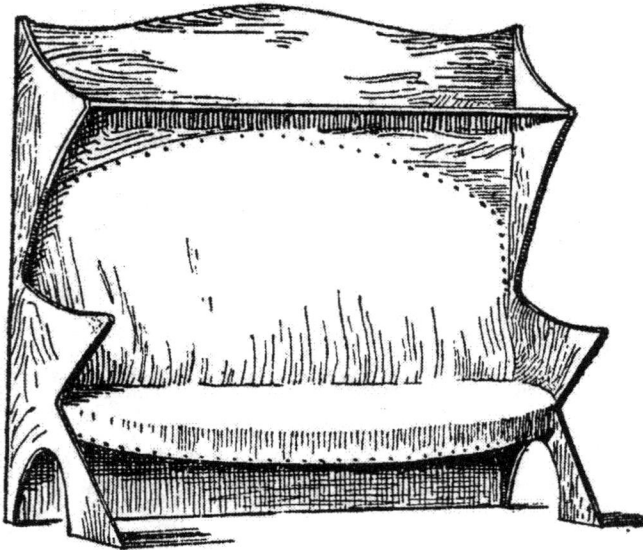

FIG. 170. NEW ART SETTEE

the man of moderate means the " real thing " in the classic styles is not always possible. The New Art offered him genuineness at a low figure and with the expenditure of comparatively little money enabled him to acquire furniture devoid of deception. It was " what it seems," and being so, in addition to pleasing his eye and fulfilling all practical requirements, he was content.

Believing that the foregoing is a correct estimate of the considerations to be taken into account in forecasting the

166

influence of the New Art furniture, we have little hesitation in saying that this style deserved the favour it won. Notwithstanding all that has been said against it, it made headway and served its purpose in shaping to some extent the development of a modern British style in furniture.

CHAPTER XIII

THE MODERN STYLE

THE two preceding chapters dealing with l'Art Nouveau and British New Art called forth some criticism when they were first published, more especially with reference to some of the views expressed with regard to l'Art Nouveau. The critics were inclined to denounce the new development, and some of them could see no element of beauty and permanence in it. The writer sees no reason to modify what he wrote on this subject a quarter of a century ago. The birth of a new style is not accomplished by deliberate effort. Evolution in furniture styles can be traced through the ages and, though periods occur where keenness hastens a movement along some particular line, the attempt to create a new style has always proved a failure.

During the last two or three years there has been a distinct move towards a new style in France and in Great Britain. The careful student will detect in what has been called the Modern Style some traces of earlier modes. It is difficult to form a reliable estimate of contemporary work. Time alone will prove to what extent the designers of the early twentieth century will produce a style that will live. At the moment, little more can be said than that pieces of peculiar beauty and elegance are being made. Novel designs executed in faultless craftsmanship and of the most carefully selected materials are being produced. Some of these, without doubt, will disappear. They present features of extravagance just as did some of the worst expressions of earlier modes. This applies even to the great Chippendale and Sheraton. But the element of real beauty is in many of the designs, and there is reason to believe that the Modern

168

Style, when it settles down, will mark a new era in furniture styles.

Perhaps the principal thing that will determine its permanency is that the designers are studying the conditions of modern life, and many of the Modern Style designs reflect modern conditions. This principle, expounded so ably by

FIG. 171. A MODERN STYLE SIDEBOARD

Morris, has an application to all the ages. It is an encouraging feature of the Modern Style that the fitness of the article for the use to which it is to be put is kept in view.

A glance at the accompanying illustrations will serve to give the reader a notion of the lines of the new style. As hitherto, the French designs are a little more daring and a good deal more elaborate than the British. In the Art Nouveau movement curves were prominent, but the characteristic of the Modern Style is plainness and simplicity.

169

This, of course, is not invariable. Moreover, the apparent simplicity of design is sometimes modified considerably by the use of less familiar and highly decorative woods. Carving is practically eliminated, but brightness and cheerfulness of colour are features of much of the furniture in this style.

In the construction of Modern Style furniture, decorative woods have been used which hitherto have found a very

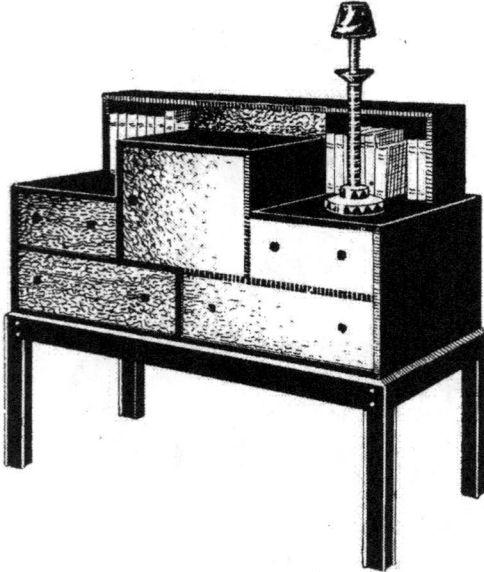

FIG. 172. A MODERN STYLE WRITING
TABLE

FIG. 173. A MODERN
STYLE CHAIR

small place in furniture construction. We may mention Macassar ebony, laurel, Indian silver-grey wood, Australian silky oak, Nigerian walnut, Bombay rosewood, Indian padauk, Canadian birch, Burmese amboyna, and African mahogany. It should be mentioned that some of these names are bestowed upon unfamiliar timbers and are not to be taken in the accepted meaning. Just as a new material was christened " artificial silk," so some of these new and beautiful

170

woods have been given names of well-known timbers, because they have presented some similar features or because no better descriptive term could be originated at the moment. In some of the new pieces, large numbers of different woods have been used, and the effect is exceedingly beautiful.

We have referred to the designers' attention to the conditions of modern life. This feature is discernible in the

FIG. 174. A MODERN STYLE DINING TABLE

designing of much of the bedroom and dining-room furniture in the Modern Style. The modern need for economizing space, coupled with the modern desire to get rid of pieces that are merely ornamental and not useful, are both reflected in the Modern Style. Fitness for its purpose is the key-note of even the most artistic models, and modern designs have certainly demonstrated the possibility of combining utility and elegance.

171

The Modern Style is too new to warrant the mention of names. Some would date its origin back to the time of William Morris, and there is no doubt that the best Morris traditions have been kept alive since the middle of the nineteenth century. Not all the efforts have been successful, but gradually the Modern Style is taking shape and settling down. So far as it is possible to form a reliable estimate of

FIG. 175. A CABINET IN THE
MODERN STYLE

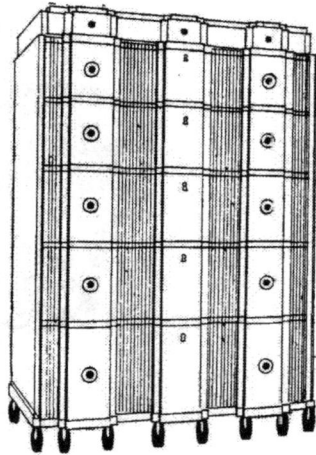

FIG. 176. A MODERN STYLE
WARDROBE

the future, it may be said that the best productions seen in the early part of the second quarter of the twentieth century will attain permanency and will rank with the best productions of the " Golden Age."

Having carefully surveyed the movement on the continent as well as in this country, the writer is of opinion that the British designers are working on the soundest lines. This is not to depreciate in any way the work of the leading continental artists and craftsmen. Some exquisite models have been produced by Parisian designers, but on the whole we

172

incline to the view that British cabinet-makers will achieve
the premier position in the Modern Style, as, in fact, they
have done in the past. The British designers always appear
to have before them the home in which the furniture will be
used. They do not seek to produce what may be described
as showroom or museum specimens, but something that will
be cherished and used in a comfortably, artistically, and
well-furnished British home.

The British designers have already been accused of something approaching a lack of enterprise, and the greater

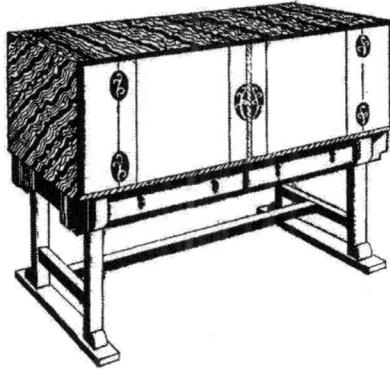

FIG. 177. A MODERN STYLE SIDEBOARD

boldness of some of the continental artists is contrasted with
the conservatism of the Britisher. Excessive courage may
amount to real rashness, and sound progress is invariably
slow. Patience and sympathy must be exercised in connection with the Modern Style. It has in it real merit, and
British artists and craftsmen have already manifested much
ability with regard to its development.

The Modern Style, if it is given adequate encouragement
by the public, is likely to rank high in the annals of furniture
production. Certainly, what has been done has proved that
the modern craftsman is in every respect equal to the
173

masters of any age, and in many respects is greatly superior. As some of the old masters suffered from lack of financial support, so will the best work of modern British craftsmen only be produced when they are maintained by a public educated to appreciate the quality rather than to dwell upon the cost of their productions.

CHAPTER XIV

HISTORY IN THE FURNITURE STYLES

IN the preceding chapters we have had occasion frequently to note the close connection it is possible to trace between the furniture styles and current history. The subject is of sufficient interest to warrant us in asking the reader's attention to a few brief illustrations showing how faithfully great social movements have been reflected in the furniture of the time. It is absolutely necessary for the proper understanding of some modes to realize their historical setting and to interpret the furniture in the light of the social condition of the people.

From the earliest times down to our own day, one steady development has been going on that has brought rich and poor nearer together so far as the requirements of their dwellings go. That feature is distinctly visible right through the centuries. The great baronial castles of feudal times have degenerated (if, indeed, degeneration is the proper word to use; it is questionable whether a " degeneration upward " is not illustrated) into the modern country houses, with their beautiful drawing-rooms and boudoirs; and from the labourer's rough shed of a cottage, with rude hewn bench, has evolved its prettily furnished, comfortable present-day equivalent, with furniture, so far as purposes of utility go, equal in every way, and often far superior, to the best that wealth can obtain. In such manner has style in furniture kept pace with the march of history. Since the Middle Ages and the Peasants' Revolt, the monopoly of privileges by the aristocracy has been steadily demolished. In proportion as the liberties of the people have increased, the authority of the hereditary lord has become lessened, until, with the growth of a democratic constitution, Jack has become very nearly as good as his master. As with Jack, so with Jack's house. In sympathy with the increasing importance of Jack, his dwelling has ever moved. His liberties and his comfortable furniture stand together. They are possessions time has won for him, and the history of his house and its contents no less than the history of his legal position and his rights of franchise, tells of his progress since the days when, as a serf, he was subject to the will of the feudal lord.

Thus, even in the reign of Elizabeth we find attempts made in the direction of introducing comfort into the cottages of the poor. It was an age of extravagance and luxuriousness, but underlying all the frivolity of the times was a seriousness on the part of the people that was apparent directly their liberties seemed to be threatened, as the Queen found on more than one occasion. Our eyes are more often turned upon the follies of the Court than upon the increasing prosperity of the common people, yet the latter was more real at this time than ever before in our history, and the reign in which our liberties may be said to have taken root is the reign that witnessed the birth of the comfortable British home.

But whilst this general movement may be traced from the earliest times, it has not proceeded without checks, and here and there the march has been arrested temporarily by local conditions. Even countries as a whole have seemed for a time to stay the forces of the evolutionary process. In social matters, periods of glorious freedom have been followed by times of great oppression, and the rigid morality of Puritanism gave way to the licentiousness of the Restoration. Even so in furniture; progress has not been without halt, and periods of rococo follow closely upon the heels of pure and classic design.

The manners and morals of the times are reflected closely

176

in contemporary arts and crafts, of which France affords us plain illustration. Consider for a moment the expensive grandeur of the Louis XIV furniture. How eloquently it tells of the times that called it forth. Follow carefully the changing styles through the reign of Louis XV, and note how unmistakably the events of the period are stamped upon its furniture. The Court is growing poorer, its public functions are conducted on a smaller scale, its tastes are less pure, its will is enfeebled, it is becoming incapable of earnestness, and its blasé life needs pampering. Every one of those features may be read in French furniture as the strength of Louis XIV gives place to the follies and vices of Louis XV and the consequent development of the rococo. Proceed and trace the coming of Louis XVI, when the Court is purged of its impurity, but is weaker than ever. Gone is the rococo, and dainty prettiness tells loudly of the effeminate character of the ruler. Then " the deluge " that was foretold, out of which comes Napoleon, like a modern Caesar, re-establishing the pure classic of Greece and Rome. It is an era of furnishing " Puritanism " in France and, like all extremes, leads to extremities of reaction, and is closely followed by the " baroque " or " debased rococo."

In England the same principle holds good. Our golden era of furniture, the time of the splendid productions of Chippendale and Sheraton, is contemporaneous with the moral, religious, and philanthropic revivals in the reign of George II. When the Wesleyans were urging the duty of earnestness and honesty, the great craftsmen we have named were preaching the same sermon no less eloquently in their enduring work. In the reign of George III the movement continues. Honest work is the key-note of the time, from statesman to workman; and the age has bequeathed to us Wedgwood and his pottery; Watt and the steam-engine; Arkwright and the spinning machine; and in furniture the work of Ince and Mayhew, Manwaring, Heppelwhite, and the brothers Adam. Green, the historian, says of the reign—

In the nation at large appeared a new moral enthusiasm.

Truly, history is to be read in manufactures as well as in books.

And what of l'Art Nouveau?

When the chief characteristics of the late nineteenth and early twentieth centuries are determined in the making of history, perhaps the two most noteworthy features will prove to be the restlessness and the boldness of the period. The most sacred things are questioned and nothing is taken for granted merely on the ground that it *has been*. The boldness that questions fearlessly the ancient traditions, that attacks laws hitherto regarded as integral parts of the Constitution, that calls upon revered institutions to justify themselves by modern arguments, is coupled with a spirit of restlessness that cries out for " something new." Clerics denounce the frivolity of the age; Conservative politicians declare that " we are all Socialists now "; artists of the old school talk bitterly of the " hooliganism " of their modern rivals.

The truth is that all see, from their different points of view, the same movement taking place. Each in his own department may check excesses, but each is powerless to stay the tide. Each may believe that he lives in a decadent age, that his is the one voice left, crying in the wilderness of modernity the message of the true prophet. Yet it is incorrect to call ours a " decadent age." On the contrary, are we not witnessing the first stages of a new renaissance, the full results of which may be enjoyed by our children's children?

Our view is that in the furniture style called l'Art Nouveau the spirit of the times, as indicated above, was accurately reflected, and in its bold restlessness we trace one more

178

illustration of the fact that the manners and customs, and even something of the temperament of a people, find expression in the decorative tendencies of the age.

The foregoing may be regarded as somewhat in the nature of a bird's-eye view of a great subject. It could be extended indefinitely, and the quest would prove both interesting and profitable. The reader, should he be so disposed, will have no difficulty in following up the suggestions in other directions. One or two further considerations arising out of the principle, however, we desire very briefly to indicate.

There are few people who have not experienced indescribable feelings akin to awe and reverence in the presence of some monumental work of antiquity. John Ruskin often refers to the sensation, as, for instance, when he wrote of the Ducal Palace (*Stones of Venice*, vol. ii)—

Sometimes when walking at evening on the Lido, whence the great chain of the Alps, crested with silver clouds, might be seen rising above the front of the Ducal Palace, I used to feel as much awe in gazing on the building as on the hills, and could believe that God had done a greater work in breathing into the narrowness of dust the mighty spirits by whom its haughty walls had been raised and its burning legends written, than in lifting the rocks of granite higher than the clouds of heaven and veiling them with their various mantle of purple flower and shadowy pine.

In that passage Ruskin beautifully indicates the real secret of our emotion in the presence of great works of art. It is not that the stones have over us some mystic power to stir our blood; it is not even that the real beauty of the work itself appeals to us. This is, of course, true, but only accounts for our feeling of admiration and the gratification of our artistic sense. The deeper sensation of awe and of reverence is attributable, as Ruskin states, to a recognition, often unconscious though it be, of the fact that these inanimate buildings carry us into the presence of human beings who lived and fought and struggled like ourselves. If we could analyse our feelings, should not we find that we are

179

awed, with thoughts not of the brick and stone, but of the hands and brains that wrought and fashioned them into shape? Great works of architecture—it is a truism—tell us eloquently of the character of the men who created them. Ruskin has worked out this idea for us. Let him put it in his own words. He writes (*On the Old Road*)—

All lovely architecture was designed for cities in cloudless air . . . cities built that men might live happily in them and take delight daily in each other's presence and powers. But our cities, built in black air which, by its accumulated foulness, first renders all ornament invisible in distance, and then chokes its interstices with soot; cities which are mere crowded masses of store and warehouse and counter, and are, therefore, to the rest of the world what the larder and cellar are to a private house; cities in which the object of men is not life, but labour; and in which all chief magnitude of edifice is to enclose machinery; cities in which the streets are not the avenues for the passing and procession of a happy people, but the drains for the discharge of a tormented mob, in which the only object in reaching any spot is to be transferred to another; . . . for a city or cities such as this no architecture is possible—nay, no desire of it is possible to their inhabitants.

We have quoted these passages because what is true of architecture is true in the domain of furniture. Ruskin has shown how history is written in the world's buildings. The same is true of the world's furniture. Have we not here some explanation of the ever-living interest manifested in the collection of old pieces of furniture to which the enthusiasm of the collector is to some extent attributable. Each genuine old chair or bureau has its tale to tell of the age that gave it birth, and of the hands that gave it shape. The emotion caused by beholding some stately cathedral or magnificent palace is closely related to the feelings that inspire the antiquarian and the connoisseur. Though they may often be unconscious of it, their pleasure in the acquisition of some fine old piece may nevertheless be assigned, in the last analysis, to that human interest in *men* that is one of the ineradicable traits of our nature. The morbid expression

180

of it is found in the eager competition often witnessed to secure the possession of something owned by a notorious criminal; the rational and healthy expression of it is to be found in the genuine love of the antique, and the desire to possess, not for mere ostentatious display, but for love of it, some link binding the present with the past.

Let us illustrate this principle in practice. A collector stands before two pieces. One is a fine old Sheraton bureau —the other a late Louis XV chair. How can he read history in the two?

The first tells its story plainly. The well-seasoned, perfectly selected wood is as good to-day as it ever was, the drawers open without careful coaxing or application of force, the doors close accurately, and even the locks remain in order. Pass your hand over the article. There are no rough edges telling of poor finish, nothing is scamped or shoddy. The bureau stands before you as fit to-day for the purpose for which it was made as the day its maker proudly gave it the finishing touch of his master hand. Its lines are beautiful, but its beauty is not divorced from utility. It fulfils all the conditions that William Morris demanded of " good citizens' furniture." It was made in an age of industrial honesty and moral enthusiasm. Examine it as closely as you will, its testimony remains unshaken. It is an honest piece of work, made by an honest man for honest men. In its production it benefited alike the man who made it and the man who bought and used it. Trade measures and social reform in Parliament and a great religious revival are the features of the age noted by the historian, and the old Sheraton bureau tells the same story to all who have eyes to read it.

Now turn to the French chair of late Louis Quinze design and you enter at once into a different atmosphere. The chair has been preserved and treasured with care, or it would not have lived so long. It was made perhaps in the same year as our Sheraton bureau, but it was made under widely different conditions. Lord Chesterfield has described the France of the time very graphically. He saw an indolent and sensual king, a depraved and cruel aristocracy, and an impoverished and ignorant lower class. There was no powerful elective parliament; the condition of the peasantry was pitiable, as added to extreme poverty, by the abuse of *lettres de cachet*, their lives and liberties were absolutely forfeited without trial or even cause being alleged. And Louis XV died, leaving the State in debt to the extent of four thousand million livres. Is not the spirit of the age " writ large " on the chair before us? It is not an honest chair. It is costly and elaborate, but it was not made because men wanted a chair on which to sit. Ostentatious display is its predominant note. The lavish excess of ornamentation and gilding tells of the blasé viciousness of the age. There is the same difference between this rococo chair and the Sheraton bureau as there is between a contemptible pander and an honest worshipper of the beautiful, and that may be said to describe the relative status of the English and French craftsman of the period.

Thus is national history written in national manufactures. If the doctrine so admirably stated by John Ruskin is true, character goes for much in matters of artistic design. He has pointed out that the Greek school of sculpture was formed during and in consequence of the national effort to discover the nature of justice; that the Tuscan movement was the same; and it is only bringing the argument up to date to apply it to all styles in furniture. We well remember being told by a well-known trade unionist that he attributed to a great extent the drunkenness and improvidence of many workmen to the fact of their being engaged in the manufacture of shoddy articles, incapable of inspiring pride or self-satisfaction. There is truth in the contention, for the

182

principle is two-edged. Whilst it is evident that the corrupt produce a corrupt art, it is also a matter of experience that men constantly employed upon unworthy tasks do themselves become degraded and corrupted. Nothing is more ennobling than honest labour; nothing more debasing than its counterfeit. Nothing exalts the craftsman more than the proud knowledge that he is doing worthy, useful, and estimable work; nothing degrades him more than to recognize that his labours are worthless and his productions contemptible. The first conditions produce the world's Sheratons. What, then, could have been the effect upon the French workmen of being under continual necessity to please the wealthy roué and the *demi-mondaine* of the eighteenth century? Let that frightful page in history, the Revolution, answer that question.

An additional interest is given to the collection of old furniture when we learn to read history from its design, material, and workmanship. And there is no period in which the social conditions of the day have not left ineradicable marks in contemporary furniture, its forms, quality, or delineation. The principle is not peculiar to furniture and decoration; it is capable of general application, and the more we study, the more convinced shall we become of its truth.

Mr. Gustav Stickley, not long ago in the *House Beautiful*, applied the principle to American furniture. After contending that "art is the true and perfect reflection of society," he goes on to show how American styles are a reflex of the restless experimenting, "spontaneous and strong," prominent in that country to-day.

The cabinet-maker . . . taking simplicity and practicality as his guides, feels that the furnishings of a farmhouse kitchen may have an artistic value far beyond those of a costly drawing-room if the latter be not wisely planned. He understands that the first and most dominant impression of beauty proceeds from the frank acknowledgment of the service to which the object is devoted.

Thus is ever produced furniture
in all respects worthy to pass into the history of art, since art is the mirror of life.

And when the furniture produced in any particular age falls short, in its workmanship or design, of the high ideal just depicted, let not the whole of the blame be thoughtlessly laid at the door of the craftsman. The national characteristics find ready expression in practical demands, which the designer must meet if he would avoid suffering martyrdom for his art. The inexorable law of supply and demand cannot be ignored, and the low standard of the artistic productions of any generation is usually to be attributed to the low artistic standard of the people generally, and not the artist in particular. Our readers will call to mind several illustrations of this in the story of the furniture styles. Chippendale was often tempted to pander to popular tastes and, in so doing, to turn his back upon what he knew to be better. The case of Sheraton is still more striking. He strove against his unappreciative public during the greater part of his life. Full of faith in the beauty and truth of his designs, he persevered in his endeavour to educate his customers. But his expenses had to be met, his family had to be provided for, and sentiments, however noble, do not satisfy the prosaic and unsentimental butcher and baker. Thus, toward the end of his career, poor Sheraton was forced to give up the struggle and capitulate to popular requirements. He put aside the work he loved, devoting himself to the more profitable occupation of producing imitations of French designs. In the light of his pathetic experience, it would be unjust to attribute the whole responsibility for the existence of inartistic productions to the artists, designers, and manufacturers, whose very existence is dependent upon the measure of favour they can secure from their patrons. The probability is that in all periods of decadence the craftsmen are unwillingly compelled to subjection and to the creation of what will sell. Periods of artistic barrenness are more often due to the absence of public appreciation of the beautiful than to the non-existence of men of ability. The age that laments its deficiency of master workers is the age in which men have lost the capacity to recognize master work. It is not enough that we build technical schools and inculcate love for the arts and crafts. We must educate that great public without whose support the veriest genius will be as a voice crying in the wilderness, and, wearying at last, will degenerate into one more producer of things that the public will buy.

In conclusion, we would emphasize the fact that by reflex action domestic art contributes in no unimportant degree to domestic morality. The influence of an artistically furnished home is invaluable, and when the craftsman makes it possible for artistic furniture to find place in the homes of the people, he serves his day and generation well indeed. Hence it behoves the decorative furnisher to study to make himself acquainted with the history of his calling. Chippendale wrote of his handicraft as a " profession," and surely he was right. Realizing all the possibilities of furnishing art, his modern confrères may well live in the same spirit, and, by faithfulness to the best traditions of the past, and to obedience to the highest modern inspirations, as veritable priests óf humanity, cultivate the flower of domestic art, until by their efforts its blossoms adorn and shed their purifying influence in the humblest dwellings. For true art is not necessarily expensive, and perhaps it is reserved for the cabinet-makers of the twentieth century to add to beauty of outline and honesty of structure the quality of economy in production which shall at last carry the treasures of decorative skill into the cottage of the peasant and the home of the artisan.

CHAPTER XV

A CHRONOLOGY OF THE FURNITURE STYLES

A BRIEF outline of the centuries is given in this chapter, in the belief that a bird's-eye view of the development of furnishing and decoration will prove useful. Only leading tendencies have been included, and the names of the most important men and events. The chapter will provide a means of ready reference from the earliest times.

THE PRE-CHRISTIAN ERA

The Egyptian is the earliest mode, and is divided into Early Egyptian (4000 B.C. to 1525 B.C.) and the Theban (1557 B.C. to 525 B.C.).

The Assyrian is dated 1270 B.C. to 625 B.C.

The Indian includes Brahman, 1400 B.C. to 500 B.C., when the Buddhist era commences.

The Etruscan (1000 B.C. to 500 B.C.).

The Persian mode (625 B.C. to 330 B.C.).

The Chinese may be dated from the time of Confucius (500 B.C.)

The Greek periods are as follows: Graeco-Pelasgic or Prehistoric (1900 B.C. to 1384 B.C.); Doric (700 B.C.); Ionic (600 B.C.); Corinthian; Hellenistic (290 B.C. to 168 B.C.).

The Roman may be dated from about 750 B.C. and the Pompeiian (pure Greek), 100 B.C.

FIRST CENTURY (A.D. 1–100)

Rome was the dominating force. Western Europe was practically barbarian, including England, France, and Germany, except so far as Roman influence had penetrated.

In Egypt Roman art flourished.

The Persian Empire had given place to the Parthian, and its art was debased Persian.

Greece was a province of Rome.

China was a great but little known nation. Much in Chinese records must be regarded as merely legendary.

In Britain the Celtic gave place to the Roman from the date of the Roman Invasion (54 B C.).

186

A CHRONOLOGY OF THE FURNITURE STYLES

SECOND CENTURY (A.D. 101–200)

Rome's sway continued over the Western nations.

The Parthians remained independent, but of little weight in matters artistic.

The European nations made gradual progress, consequent upon increasing familiarity with the Romans' manners and customs.

THIRD CENTURY (A.D. 201–300)

Rome's art became luxurious. The conflict between pagan and Christian became more intense, and increasing dangers were experienced from the Barbarians of the North, who constantly threatened invasion, and obtained local successes. The Barbarians had no art.

The Parthian Empire had given way to the Sassanian, whose art was Persian.

The Europeans steadily progressed along Roman lines.

FOURTH CENTURY (A.D. 301–400)

Rome became Christian (nominally) in the reign of Constantine, and Byzantium (Constantinople) became the capital of the Roman Empire (A.D. 330). The Byzantine dates from this period.

Europe progressed considerably, its development being hastened by missionary zeal on the part of Roman Christians, who dispatched preachers.

FIFTH CENTURY (A.D. 401–500)

The Roman Empire fell (A.D. 476) under attacks by the Northern Barbarians. Great destruction of works of art took place. The Roman style became the Romanesque, a Byzantine corruption of pure Roman.

Europe adopted the Romanesque toward the end of this century. Ireland was still Celtic.

The dominating influence of the century was the Byzantine.

SIXTH CENTURY (A.D. 501–600)

The Romanesque style was still the dominant one.

Europe developed the Romanesque.

The Byzantine was now in its prime. The birth of Mohammed (A.D. 571) marks the commencement of the Mohammedan and Saracenic nations.

SEVENTH CENTURY (A.D. 601–700)

The Byzantine continued to flourish, though in frequent danger from the Saracens, whose strongholds were in Arabia. Before the death of

187

A CHRONOLOGY OF THE FURNITURE STYLES

Mohammed (A.D. 632), the Saracenic, or Moorish, style was commenced.

Europe was still Romanesque.

EIGHTH CENTURY (A.D. 701–800)

The Romanesque flourished in France and Italy.
The Moors conquered Spain, and Moorish style rapidly developed.
The Saxon flourished in England.
The Byzantine flourished in the East and spread to Russia.

NINTH CENTURY (A.D. 801–900)

The Moors continued to hold Spain. The Moorish style developed.
England continued Saxon.
The Romanesque continued to flourish in France and Italy.
The Byzantine continued to flourish in the East and in Russia.
Germany and Flanders became independent Powers. In both the art was Romanesque.

TENTH CENTURY (A.D. 901–1000)

The Moors continued supreme in Spain.
The Saxons continued supreme in England.
The Romanesque held sway in France.
The Russian Byzantine gave way to a new style formed by a combination of Byzantine and Celtic, the latter being introduced into the country by Irish Christian missionaries.
The pure Byzantine developed into the late or Italian style.

ELEVENTH CENTURY (A.D. 1001–1100)

The Romanesque style continued to flourish in France and Italy, though Spanish influence extended to France, leading to the adoption of Moorish details.
The Byzantine continued to flourish in the East.
The Moorish in Spain entered its best period in this century, and the style remained the dominant one, though the entrance of Christianity into the northern part of the kingdom led to the introduction of the Romanesque.
The Norman Conquest (1066) led to the introduction of the Romanesque into England. Bayeux tapestry, wrought by Matilda of Flanders, wife of William the Conqueror.

TWELFTH CENTURY (A.D. 1101–1200)

Byzantine in the East.
The Moorish flourished in Spain.

188

A CHRONOLOGY OF THE FURNITURE STYLES

The Early English style—a crude Gothic (1189).
French Gothic commenced in the latter half of this century.

THIRTEENTH CENTURY (A.D. 1201–1300)

Byzantine in the East.
Moorish still flourished in Spain. Alhambraic during this century.
French Gothic developed.

FOURTEENTH CENTURY (A.D. 1301–1400)

Byzantine in the East, but weakening.
The Moorish still flourished in Spain, though in the North the Gothic
gained increasing influence.
Dutch (1383–1750).
Decorated Gothic or Ornamental English style (1307).
Perpendicular or Florid Gothic (1399).
In France the style was Gothic. Tapestry weaving introduced toward
the end of this century.
The Gothic style flourished in Italy.

FIFTEENTH CENTURY (A.D. 1401–1500)

Byzantine (to 1453). The Turkish followed the Byzantine.
Moorish (to 1492).
Italian Renaissance (a variation of the Byzantine).
Venetian Renaissance (1490).
Roman Renaissance (1444). Originated with Donato Lazzari, followed
by Giacomo Barozzio (1507). Supreme period reached in Michael
Angelo Buonarotti (1474).

SIXTEENTH CENTURY (A.D. 1501–1600)

The Arabian (1500–1699).
German Renaissance (1550).
Spanish Renaissance (1500), Hispano-Moresque.
Flemish (1507–1750).
Venetian Renaissance (Palladio, 1518).
The Tudor or English Renaissance (1509). Introduced by John of Padua,
architect to Henry VIII. Tapestry making introduced into England.
The Elizabethan style (1558). Dutch influence became apparent. (Henry
VIII, 1509–1547; Edward VI, 1547–1553; Mary, 1553–1558; Eliza-
beth, 1558–1603.)
French Renaissance (1515). A freely ornamented Gothic, introduced by
Fra Giacondo, about 1502, in the reign of Louis XII. (Louis XII,
1498–1515; François I, 1515–1547; Henri II, 1547–1559; François II,
1559–1560; Charles IX, 1560–1574; Henri III, 1374–1589; Henri IV,
1589–1610.)

A CHRONOLOGY OF THE FURNITURE STYLES

SEVENTEENTH CENTURY (A.D. 1601–1700)

Arabian ends (1699).

The Jacobean style (1603). Italian influence appeared. Mortlake tapestry manufactory established (1619). (James I, 1603–1625; Charles I, 1625–1649.)

The Cromwellian style (1653). (The Commonwealth, 1653–1659; Charles II, 1660–1685; James II, 1685–1689.)

The William and Mary style (1689). Dutch furniture largely imported. (William and Mary, 1689–1702.)

Italian Renaissance, followed by rococo styles.

Louis XIV style (1643). The Gobelins and Beauvais factories established. Rococo style appeared (1690). The era of Charles Le Brun, André Charles Boulle, Jean Berain, Jean Le Pautre, Daniel Marot. (Louis XIII, 1610–1643; Louis XIV, 1643–1715.)

EIGHTEENTH CENTURY (A.D. 1701–1800)

The Queen Anne style. Dutch influence still apparent (1702–1714).

The Georgian period. Era of the greatest British furniture designers. Inigo Jones (1744), H. Copeland (1746), Thomas Sheraton (1751), Thomas Chippendale (1754), Ince and Mayhew (1760), Manwaring (1766), R. and J. Adam (1773), M. A. Pergolesi (1777), Heppelwhite & Co. (1789). (George I, 1714–1727; George II, 1727–1760; George III, 1760–1820.)

The Regency in France (1715–1723) Philip, Duc d'Orleans, Regent (died 1723).

Louis XV style. Rococo period. Leading men : Watteau, Nicholas Pineau, Jacques Caffieri, Jules Aurèle Meissonnier, Jacques Blondel, Denizol, Charles Cressent, Oeben, Tessier, Martin. (Louis XV, 1723–1774.)

Louis XVI style. Leading men: David Roentgen, Riesener, Gouthière. (Louis XVI, 1774–1792, Marie Antoinette, Queen.)

The Directoire style. (Republic, 1792; the Directoire, 1795–1799; the Consulate, 1799–1804, Napoleon, Consul.)

NINETEENTH CENTURY (A.D. 1801–1900)

Victorian style (1837).

New Art style, about 1885. (George IV, 1820–1830; William IV, 1830–1837; Victoria, 1837–1901; Edward VII, 1901.)

The Empire style. David appointed by Napoleon. Jacob Desmalter, *ébéniste*. Percier, architect. (Napoleon I, 1804–1814.)

Modern French styles (1871).

L'Art Nouveau (about 1885).

INDEX

191

INDEX